Temptation in the Archives

Temptation in the Archives

Essays in Golden Age Dutch Culture

Lisa Jardine

First published in 2015 by
UCL Press
University College London
Gower Street
London WC1E 6BT

Freely available online at: www.ucl.ac.uk/ucl-press

A CIP catalogue record for this book is available
from The British Library.

ISBN: 978-1-910634-02-8 (Hbk.)
ISBN: 978-1-910634-03-5 (Pbk.)
ISBN: 978-1-910634-09-7 (PDF)
ISBN ebook: 978-1-910634-07-3 (epub)
ISBN ebook: 978-1-910634-08-0 (mobi)
DOI:10.14324/111.9781910634035

For Arnoud Visser
Amicus est tamquam alter idem

Preface

In spring 2013, the Rijksmuseum in Amsterdam – home to unimaginable treasures from the Dutch Golden Age – reopened after a ten-year closure for refurbishment. Strolling through opulent rooms displaying towering blue-and-white pyramidal delftware tulip vases, gorgeous jewel-like paintings by Vermeer and Rembrandt, and ornately inlaid baroque furniture a week after the reopening, I came upon an object which for me went to the heart of the seventeenth-century cultural relationship between England and the Netherlands. If only I had known of it a few years earlier, when I was writing my book-length study of Anglo-Dutch relations in the seventeenth century, *Going Dutch*. I would certainly have reproduced it there.

In a quite large glass display case all of its own sat a small rectangular block of mottled grey stone, in a modest-sized, purpose-made wooden box. Two original hand-written labels, in a rather unconfident cursive hand, in fading brown ink, are affixed – one inside the box's lid, the other pasted on to the stone itself. 'A piece of the Rock on which William Prince of Orange first set foot on landing at Brixham in Torbay Nov[embe]r 4th 1688', the latter reads.[1]

The fragment of stone in its contemporary setting reminded me powerfully of a similar fragment of stone on my own bookshelf – a piece of the Berlin Wall, given to me by a friend who had raced from London to Berlin in November 1989, to witness the 'people power'

---

1 The inscription inside the lid reads: 'The Stone on which King William III first placed his foot on landing in England was long preserved in Old Market House of Brixham, and when placed in the Obelisk now on the Pier a piece of it was kept by the Harbour Master & afterwards given to me & now placed in this box of heart of English Oak for Her Majesty the Queen of Holland. R. Fenwick Elrington Vicar of Lower Brixham Nov 4. 1868.'

which brought down the barrier between East and West in that city. Like the resident of Brixham, I cherish that small relic (complete with an obliging East German guard's ink stamp on it) as a reminder of a twentieth-century life-changing moment – an emotional turning-point for many of us caught up in the European politics of the time, as well as a landmark historical event.

The little box in the Rijksmuseum is lasting testimony to the fact that for its original owner, the moment when a Dutch Stadholder set foot on English soil was similarly charged with emotion, and similarly recognised from the instant it happened as reshaping the lives of both the English and the Dutch.

Standing in front of that glass case – and I returned to it several times that morning during the hours I spent wandering through the bright, airy rooms of the Rijksmuseum – I was struck by how vivid material objects make historical events. In my own work it is generally an archival document, handled and deciphered for the first time, that gives me the particular thrill of connecting with the distant past. Arlette Farge captures the tingling excitement of a fragment of parchment or a bundle of papers in her *Allure of the Archives*, which is a book I treasure and to which I regularly return.

I also realised from my encounter with the Brixham stone fragment how strongly I feel emotionally about events in the Netherlands and in England in the seventeenth century. We are all still complicit, I believe, in a pact sealed partly publicly, partly socially and privately, between the Dutch and ourselves during those eventful decades. I still detect today, in the easy relationship between my graduate students and their counterparts in Leiden and Utrecht when we visit, a sharing of cultural outlook and intellectual convictions which continues to shape their attitudes and beliefs. It is not just an educational context that they share, but also taste in gardening and cooking.

It is no accident, I feel, that both countries look back to a golden age, an age of Imperialism, an age when their interventions counted on the world stage, and that the two nations share today a mutual unease about loss of power and influence, and uncertainty about their role in a global political arena. Yet the rich cultural heritages of both continue to hold sway worldwide, and hordes of international visitors flock to their great national museums.

Have I confessed to more emotional investment in things Anglo-Dutch than is proper for a professional historian? Perhaps. The essays that follow are scrupulous exercises in historical investigation, which craft the evidence I uncover into narratives designed to shine a vivid light on those similarities between English and Dutch cultures to which I am so committed. Readers may decide for themselves whether they are prepared to follow me on my journey into the nooks and crannies of Anglo-Dutch history. I would also encourage them to keep an eye out for the moments at which I see lessons to be learned for the Europe of today in the international cultural exchanges of the past.

Each of the essays here was written for a particular public occasion, either in England or the Netherlands. 'Temptation in the archives' was my inaugural lecture at University College London, where I have been happily ensconced since autumn 2012. 'Never trust a pirate' first saw the light of day as the 2006 Roy Porter memorial lecture for the Wellcome Trust, 'The reputation of Sir Constantijn Huygens' was the formal KB lecture I delivered at the Koninklijke Bibliotheek in The Hague, at the end of my term as KB Fellow at the Netherlands Institute for Advanced Study in the Humanities and Social Sciences (NIAS) in 2008. The research for 'Dear Song' was also carried out during the tenure of my KB Fellowship, working with the invaluable archival resources of the KB in The Hague, under the benevolent eye of their curator, Dr Ad Leerintveld. It was first delivered at a conference at the University of Amsterdam, though it has, I hope, benefited from further research and thought, as well as dialogue with students and faculty in the UK and the Netherlands since. '1688 and all that' was first delivered as the Cundill lecture at McGill University in 2010, one of the public events associated with my winning the Cundill Prize in 2009. 'The Afterlife of Homo Ludens' was the Huizinga Lecture at the University of Leiden, and described by that university as the 'mother of all lectures'. It is delivered from the pulpit of the vast Pieterskerk in Leiden, which is lit by hundreds of flickering candles, in front of an audience of 900 people.

The variety and sometimes grandeur of these occasions provided me with a platform on which to perform with intensity – for every lecture is a performance – the beliefs and understanding of the past I have acquired over many years in academic life. Yet precisely because they began life on a public stage, they try to carry their scholarly burden lightly, and to concentrate on enthralling an audience that might otherwise not find time to muse on the scraps of paper I have uncovered in dusty archives on either side of the Narrow Sea.

Acknowledgements

I owe so many debts to colleagues and friends who have helped me with the thinking behind this volume of essays that I hardly know where to start. By this stage in my career, the debts to others have mounted up into mountain ranges. The solution seems to be to limit myself here to thanking those without whom this project could simply never have happened.

First and foremost among these is former President and Provost of UCL, Malcolm Grant, who offered me and my research Centre for Editing Lives and Letters a home in 2012 when we were homeless. Without him my career could not have continued so happily, and there would be no book of essays. His successor, Michael Arthur, has been equally warm in his welcome, and has encouraged me in every project CELL and I have embarked on since we arrived, including the present one.

To the librarians, archivists, scholars and graduate students who have contributed to *Temptation in the Archives*, you all know who you are, and I hope I have been consistent in footnoting my gratitude in the text wherever you helped me. Most notably, in the Netherlands, Ad Leerintveld, Nadine Akkerman, Arnoud Visser, Marika Keblusek and Jan van der Motten have helped and supported my Low Countries work.

UCL Press staff have been immensely supportive and helpful in bringing this, their first publication, to fruition. Any remaining errors in the text are, of course, all my own fault. My agent Toby Mundy helped me sort out the complexities of open access publication.

Above all, my colleagues at CELL and my graduate students past and present have provided the kind of support that most people can only dream of. So it is to Robyn Adams, Matt Symonds, Lucy Stagg, Jaap Geraerts, Louisiane Ferlier, James Everest, Brooke Palmieri, Helen

Graham-Matheson, Nydia Pineda and Amanda Brunton that I extend my most heartfelt and warmest thanks. You are always there for me, and I couldn't do it without you.

As for my immediate family, there are no words adequately to capture all that I owe to them.

A word on the structure of this book. Many of the sources I use are inaccessible to any but privileged scholars, fragile documents hidden in libraries closed to the general reader. I have chosen to reproduce almost all my transcriptions of documents I have consulted, here as appendices, in the hope that some readers may choose to take the research I have undertaken further, to discover exciting further features of early modern Anglo-Dutch culture. Hopefully, this will make this an 'open access' book in the fullest sense.

April 2015

Contents

1
Temptation in the Archives

This is the story of a paper-chase – a seemingly fruitless search in the archives, which eventually yielded a seventeenth-century letter I had been trying to find for several years. It is a cautionary tale about the trust we historians place in documents and records, and how badly we want each precious piece of evidence to add to the historical picture. And it is a story which illustrates in a number of ways the essential *uncertainty* which underlies, and ultimately gives purpose to, archival research in the humanities – in spite of the reassuring materiality of the hundreds-of-years-old piece of paper we hold in our hand.

***

In 2009, at the end of a period working on seventeenth-century Holland for my book *Going Dutch*, I took up a Fellowship at the Royal Library in The Hague, working on their large holding of the correspondence of Sir Constantijn Huygens. While researching his early career I came across a sequence of almost-illegible letters in French, exchanged in the 1620s between Huygens and someone he addressed – with some familiarity – as 'Mademoiselle Croft' (or occasionally just as 'Croft'). The letters piqued my curiosity – not least because the assiduous editor of Huygens's substantial surviving correspondence, J. A. Worp, had chosen not to transcribe them in full in his 'complete' edition. As for Croft, nobody of that name had figured anywhere in any of the Huygens materials I had read until then.

Born in 1596, Constantijn Huygens was a Dutch polymath diplomat, poet and musician, who, as personal secretary to the Stadholder, Frederik Hendrik, is acknowledged to have played a prominent part in the artistic and cultural flowering at the court in the northern Netherlands of Frederik Hendrik and his wife Amalia von Solms in the decades following the death of his half-brother, the previous Stadholder, Maurits of Nassau in 1625. Although Sir Constantijn is little appreciated here in Britain, he has a formidable reputation in the Netherlands, where he is regarded as almost single-handedly having been responsible for raising the international profile of the court of Frederik Hendrik and Amalia in The Hague, transforming it into one of the most celebrated in Europe for its cultivation, artistic splendour and general ostentation and glamour.

Electronic resources enables trawling systematically for evidence of individuals to yield a richer haul of relevant documents and references today than in those when we had to rely on writing formal letters of inquiry to the custodians of local archives to request information. Yet I could find nothing about Margaret Croft beyond the fact that she had been a maid of honour to Elizabeth of Bohemia, sister of Charles I and wife of Frederick, Elector Palatine.

So it was natural that I should consult the acknowledged expert on Elizabeth of Bohemia, Dr Nadine Akkerman, who as well as editing the three volumes of Elizabeth's letters, is embarking on a much-anticipated modern biography for Oxford University Press. She pointed me in the direction of an obscure 1909 biography of the Queen of Bohemia in which Margaret Croft's name does occur a number of times: Mary Anne Everett Green's *Elizabeth Electress Palatine and Queen of Bohemia* (an expanded reissue of a brief biographical essay Green had first published in 1855).[1]

Croft appears several times in Green's book, which, after the fashion of its age, has what to us feels like a slightly saccharine, sentimental tone to its conscientious excavation of the lives of prominent ladies from the historical archives. Croft attracts Green's attention both because of her amorous adventures at court and because she was deemed to be the author of a significant letter, chronicling an important Dutch 'royal tour', which took place in 1625. Green writes 'During the summer of 1625 the King and Queen [of Bohemia] with the Princess of Orange [Amalia von Solms], undertook a journey into North Holland. [A] record of their excursion . . . was written by a young lady of the Court [Margaret Croft].'[2]

---

1 It is in fact a revised edition by Green's niece of a shorter 'Life' of Elizabeth, published by Green in 1855 as one of the lives of royal women in her six-volume work, *Lives of the Princesses of England*.
2 M. A. E. Green, *Elizabeth Electress Palatine and Queen of Bohemia*, revised by her niece S. C. Lomas (London: Methuen & Co., 1909), p. 245.

As far as I am aware, this is the only eye-witness account of a 'triumphal tour' taken by the new Dutch Stadholder and his (also new) wife, together with Elizabeth and Frederick of Bohemia. Green's selective quotations from this letter were tantalisingly vivid. I made a note to follow up this one substantial piece of evidence directly involving Croft at a later date.

***

There is no portrait of Madge Crofts (as Elizabeth of Bohemia affectionately calls her), as far as I can discover. We can, however, see ladies very like her from Elizabeth of Bohemia's court circle in a book of watercolour sketches of the Northern Netherlands made in the 1620s, which includes several 'from life' studies of Elizabeth of Bohemia and Amalia von Solms and their entourages.[3]

The closest we have to an actual physical glimpse of her – a unique trace of her hand on paper – is a note in The National Archives at Kew, where it is catalogued as 'possibly to Lord Conway' (I cannot find out on what basis).

The note reads: 'I beseech yo[ur] Lo[rdship] to reade this inclosed and let me know yo[u]r pleasure, Yo[u]r most humble and most obedient seruant Marg[are]t Croft'.[4]

As a start, I think this nicely conveys a possible role for Margaret as intermediary and facilitator: she passes a written communication to an English nobleman, and offers her services to carry out its instructions.

Margaret appears to have come over to The Hague with the English Ambassador Sir Dudley Carleton's wife in 1623 and to have joined the household of the exiled Queen Elizabeth of Bohemia (Charles I's sister, who was, of course, herself English by birth) a year later.[5] She is associated (mostly by hearsay) with a number of sentimental scandals at the court of Elizabeth of Bohemia, of which more shortly. In 1637 she fell out with Princess Elizabeth, the Queen's eldest daughter, and was 'let go' while on a visit to England. Queen Elizabeth lobbied her brother Charles I and other prominent English court figures such as Archbishop

---

3 M. Royalton-Kisch (ed.), *Adriaen van de Venne's Album in the Department of Prints and Drawings in the British Museum* (London: British Museum Publications, 1988).

4 SP 16/530 f. 10 Date [Jan] 1629.

5 'I wish you could speak to the queen about [Bessy Dohna], to know what you may trust to, for Mrs Crofts is to come over with me; her mother and she were here with me, the queen said she would take them both [Mrs Crofts and Bessy Dohna] together' (Lady Carleton to Sir D. Carleton, 8 June 1623. Cit. Green, *Elizabeth Electress Palatine* p. 250, n. 3).

Laud by letter to have Margaret paid a considerable sum as compensation for her thirteen years' service.[6]

In her biography of Elizabeth of Bohemia, Green tells us that in November 1625, the Queen (an inveterate match-maker) made serious attempts to broker a marriage between Margaret Croft and Henry Erskine, younger son of the Scottish Earl of Marr. Elizabeth wrote to the Earl, in a letter delivered by his son, returning from what had evidently been an enjoyable sojourn at the Palatine Court in The Hague, as follows:

> I cannot lett your worthie sonne returne to you without these lines, to continue you the assurance of my affection. He will acquaint you with a business that neerlie concernes him, which is an affection he hath taken to a gentlewoman that serves me; whom he desires with your consent, to make his wife. . . . For the gentlewoman, Crofts, I can assure you she is an honest discreet woman and doth carie herself verie well. If I had not this good opinion of her, I should not intreate you, as I doe by these, that you will give him your consent to marrie her.[7]

In spite of Elizabeth's assurance that 'he hath not made anie acquainted with it because you shoulde know it first', and that she herself 'came to the knowledge of it by chaunce, for seing him much with her I did suspect it, and asking him the question he confest to me his love', this affair had surely come to the attention of the court in The Hague.

We do not know what the Earl of Marr's response was to this letter, but we can be certain that a family as close to the Scottish and English thrones as the Marrs would not have countenanced a marriage to a non-noble maid of honour – not even for a younger son by a second marriage.[8] We may assume, therefore, that Margaret

6 For the events surrounding Margaret's pensioning off, see the letter to Elizabeth from her son Charles Louis, Elector Palatine, of 3 June 1637. N. Akkerman (ed.), *The Correspondence of Elizabeth Stuart, Queen of Bohemia*, Volume II, 1632–1642 (Oxford: Oxford University Press, 2011), p. 604. [See also references in Volume 2 of Elizabeth of Bohemia's correspondence, passim.]

7 Cit. Green, *Elizabeth Electress Palatine*, p. 423. Elizabeth wrote to the Countess of Marr in similar terms.

8 According to the *DNB*: 'In 1617 Mar snapped up the heiress to the earldom of Buchan as a wife for his eldest son by his second marriage, James, but this seems to have brought more costs than benefits. He also spent much on assembling a barony of Cardross in Stirlingshire for Henry, his next son, in the 1600s. On 10 June 1610 Mar was created Lord Cardross, being empowered to transfer that title to Henry. In January 1624 he sought to buy Henry a place in the privy chamber, but the expected vacancy failed to arise. He tried to prevent Henry's intended marriage in 1623–4, but, as Kellie commented to him, Henry "is willfull,

TEMPTATION IN THE ARCHIVES

had been associated with Henry Erskine for some time at Elizabeth's court, and that their relationship was court gossip. When permission for the marriage was not forthcoming, her reputation must surely have suffered. Subsequently, her name is associated romantically with a number of prominent figures in Dutch court circles.

***

Constantijn Huygens had probably made Margaret Croft's acquaintance when he took up his new post as Secretary to Frederik Hendrik in April 1625 and moved from the bourgeoisie into court circles in The Hague. In 2009–10 I was interested in a decorous, semi-formal and chaste series of epistolary exchanges between Huygens and a young woman named Dorothea van Dorp – a neighbour in the élite Het Plein district, a childhood friend and reputedly his fiancée. What I found remarkable about the fragmentary correspondence with Margaret Croft was how markedly it differed in tone and content from the Van Dorp correspondence.[9]

The first of his surviving notes to Croft is dated (in Huygens's hand, in the margin of the draft) 5 August 1627, 'devant Groll' [outside Grolle] – that is, during the annual summer military campaign against the French on which Huygens accompanied the Stadholder.[10] Its tone is flirtatious and conspiratorial – perhaps surprisingly, considering that Constantijn had been married for little more than four months at the time. Huygens suggests that he has been encouraged to write because the Count of Hanau – by insinuation, Margaret's lover or protector – has taken him into his confidence.[11]

Over the next several months, Huygens keeps Margaret Croft informed of the fact that intercepted letters threaten to make known some 'indiscretion' and damage to her and others' reputations, and implies that only his own intervention will keep the matter from public

wherein he showes himselfe to be a wadge of the rycht tree, that is of your selfe" (Mar and Kellie MSS, 2.191).' Julian Goodare, 'Erskine, John, eighteenth or second earl of Mar (c. 1562–1634)', *Oxford Dictionary of National Biography*, Oxford University Press, 2004; online edn, May 2006, http://www.oxforddnb.com/view/article/8867. It looks as though it may have been Henry Erskine who was in the Netherlands in 1624–5. See *DNB* entry for William Douglas, seventh earl of Morton (1582–1648), which names Henry Erskine as accompanying Douglas on a grand tour of the continent. All John Marr's children made suitable marriages to Scottish nobility.

9 See Chapter 5, 'Dear Song', below pp. 65–83.
10 These campaigns were part of the Thirty Years War.
11 KB KA XLIX-1 f. 375. See also Worp, letter number 695 [not transcribed] 'Evenals gij, voel ik het verlies van den dapperen edelman, nu onlangs bij dit beleg gesneuveld. De graaf van Hanau heeft geweten, welke gevoelens ik jegens u koesterde Le 2e d'Aoust 1632.' [This is the same letter as 364.]

knowledge. There is little doubt that he intends to suggest that favours are owed by Mademoiselle Croft to himself, for his services in interceding in this way. Such favours may indeed have been forthcoming – a letter in the same run, written to her much later, in 1633, implies familiarity, not only between Constantijn and Margaret, but also between her and his sister Constantia, and closes in terms of intense affection.

The tone of these letters is teasing and familiar. It suggests that the court circles of the Stadholder and the King and Queen of Bohemia were worlds away from the decorous middle-class salons of Huygens and his literary friends like P. C. Hooft, whose exchanges of letters with educated artistic Dutch women have been closely studied by historians like myself.

This, then, was the context in which I encountered and became intrigued by Madge Croft. To be honest, although I wrote and published a paper which included the correspondence to which I have just alluded (my paper on Dorothea van Dorp), Croft remained a puzzle to me, and I continued to worry that the scribbled notes I had transcribed did not contain enough of substance to allow me to understand the circumstances under which they were written, nor to do justice to the relationship – whatever that really was – between Margaret and Constantijn.[12]

***

So now let's go back to that letter I was so anxious to find in the archives, the one Green had seen in the Public Record Office (as the The National Archives [TNA] then was), and which she associated with Madge Croft and her activities at the court of Elizabeth of Bohemia.

Green's scrupulously archivally based biography of Elizabeth of Bohemia quotes selectively from a letter in French written by Margaret Croft in summer 1625 and intercepted on its way to her cousin in England. The letter is an eye-witness account, chronicling events on a celebratory tour of North Holland, taken by the 'royal' ladies of the courts at The Hague – Elizabeth of Bohemia, Amalia von Solms and their entourages. It apparently circulated widely that autumn under the title 'Copie d'une lettre interceptée et dechiffrée en passant entre une des dames d'honneur de la reyne de Boheme et une demoiselle sa cousine en Angleterre'. I think we can safely attribute the letter to Margaret Croft. Sir George Goring wrote to the English Ambassador Sir Dudley Carleton on 8 September 1625 that a response to this letter was

---

12 One of the problems with these notes is that Huygens's French is deliberately cryptic, so that it is extremely hard to construe, even once deciphered.

in the process of being written (possibly ghosted by himself), for which his intimate friend 'Mage Crofts' need only wait a week:

> But more of this in the answer to the Queen of Bohemia's damoyselle that wrote the voyadge of North Holland, for which I beseech your lordship believe her cossen here shall not be unthankfull. . . . I pray you, my lord, commande my goshippe [gossip] and fellow Mage Crofts to forgive me but till next week.[13]

Spring 1625 was a momentous time at the English and Dutch courts. On 27 March (early April by continental calculation) the English king, James I, had died, to be succeeded by his son Charles I, Elizabeth of Bohemia's devoted brother, and a strong supporter of the Protestant Palatinate cause for which her father had systematically refused to give political or military support. This in spite of his daughter's passionate epistolary entreaties for him to help restore her and her husband to their former territories (seized by the Catholic Hapsburg Emperor Ferdinand in 1620).[14] In the Netherlands, Stadholder Maurits had died without issue on 23 April (though he had plenty of offspring, he had never married). On his deathbed Maurits had insisted that his half-brother Frederik Hendrik marry his current mistress Amalia von Solms, chief maid of honour to Elizabeth of Bohemia, to ensure the continuity of the Nassau line. Sir Constantijn Huygens successfully lobbied to become Frederik Hendrik's first secretary under the new regime, before the end of April.

That summer, Amalia van Solms, the new Stadholder's new wife, together with Elizabeth of Bohemia (her former employer), toured North Holland in triumph, to celebrate Amalia's meteoric rise from one of Elizabeth's ladies-in-waiting to Princess of Orange, and the fact that Elizabeth's brother Charles I was now King of England, giving the Bohemian exiles more status and, they hoped, significant influence in the Protestant political league in mainland Europe. It was a joyous trip, full of expectation and excitement, and (to judge from the brief extracts quoted by Green) its jubilant atmosphere was vividly captured in Margaret Croft's intercepted letter.

It has to be said, however, that in her biography of the Queen of Bohemia Green sounds a little reluctant about having to rely on this particular document:

---

13   Cit. Green, *Elizabeth Electress Palatine*, p. 245, n. 2.
14   An Imperial edict formally deprived Frederick of the Palatinate in 1623.

As the record of [Elizabeth of Bohemia and Amalia von Solms']
excursion, though minute, was written by a young lady of the
Court [Margaret Croft], whose only thought was amusement, we
must be content with such details as are afforded in her sprightly
narrative, from which all serious subjects are banished.

It is a pity (reading between the lines, we can hear Green saying)
that this eye-witness account of an important otherwise-unrecorded
journey is written in such a frivolous fashion, thereby detracting from
the fundamental seriousness of the occasion. The frivolity is to be
contrasted with (say) the published accounts of the lavish occasions
along the route of the journey Elizabeth of Bohemia had made in 1613
for her marriage to Frederick.

So I set off to decide about the contents of the letter for myself. In
late 2010, with Green's State Papers Holland reference number in the
(now) TNA, my colleague at the Centre for Editing Lives and Letters, Dr
Robyn Adams and I went in search of Margaret Croft's letter. We spent a
long, frustrating and fruitless day there, in spite of the fact that we were
ably assisted by TNA's ever-helpful staff, and failed to find any trace of
the letter we were looking for. Yet all of us were convinced that it must
be there somewhere. All of us were confident that Green must have seen
the document, and equally sure that a document once in the TNA would
never have been destroyed – it will simply have been misplaced.

I began to suspect it had been misplaced deliberately. Green had
clearly been disconcerted by the contents of the letter, and its 'sprightly'
tone – unseemly perhaps, coming from a lady of Elizabeth's court.
Perhaps she had cannily lodged it out of place in the archive, where it
was safe, but where the curious could only find it again with difficulty.

Then, in August 2012, Nadine Akkerman emailed me to say she
had come across a published transcription of the Croft letter, quite by
chance. It was included as an appendix to Martin Royalton-Kisch's 1988
facsimile edition of Adriaen van der Venne's 1620s watercolour picture
album, to which I referred earlier. Royalton-Kisch made nothing at all
of the letter (indeed, did not translate it from the original French), but
gave the correct State Papers reference – one whole volume away from
the one on which Robyn Adams and I had based our search. Instead
of being in State Papers Holland, Margaret Croft's letter was in State
Papers German:

The National Archives, State Papers German 81/33 folios 147–50.
Calendar entry title: 'Queen of Bohemia's Maid of Honour to a

Cousin. Endorsement fo. 150v: "Copie d'vne lettre jnterceptée & deschiffrée en passant entre vne des filles d'honneur de la Royne de Boheme, & vne Damoisselle sa Cousine en Angleterre".'[15]

Within days Nadine had retrieved scans of the letter and emailed them to me – Oh! the joys of the State Papers online – and I had translated it. You can imagine our excitement. Were we finally going to be able to unravel the mystery of the strikingly active, manipulative role Margaret Croft appeared to play in the lives of several influential men at the courts of England and the Netherlands?[16] Would the letter explain the innuendo in Constantijn Huygens's notes to Margaret Croft?

***

The answer turned out to be a resounding 'No'. But before I explain further, I need to pause here to explain why I was so confident that the informant on Margaret Croft to whom Nadine Akkerman had originally directed my attention – Mary Anne Everett Green – was to be taken extremely seriously.

Green is a figure of iconic status for anyone who works on the State Papers Domestic in the TNA. She was one of a band of Victorian women historians who worked assiduously in the archives, retrieving the buried traces of women's writing from under the mountains of correspondence exchanged through official and unofficial channels by prominent men. Her reputation for accuracy was legendary – it can be tracked through all the adulatory reviews of the published volumes of the Calendars of State Papers Domestic as they were issued in the late nineteenth century. When I had suggested that Green might have deliberately misplaced the Croft letter among the State Papers, I was encouraged in this surmise by the early modern records specialist at the TNA, Dr Katy Mair (a CELL graduate). She had told

15 Green said it was in 'S. P. Holland, 1625' (p. 245, n. 2). In Green's niece's preface to the revised edition of *Elizabeth Electress Palatine and Queen of Bohemia*, she explains that she has done her best to check all the references to State Papers Foreign, since the calendars for these were not produced until after Green's death: 'In preparing the "Life of Elizabeth of Bohemia" for the press, I have tried to do just what I believe my aunt would have done if she had herself issued a new edition. That is, I have corrected any inaccuracies detected in the text, have added here and there short notes, where new light has been shed on the subject, and have (so far as possible) identified and modernized the very numerous references to the Foreign and Departmental State Papers, now all at the Public Record Office. These papers have been entirely re-arranged since the Life of Elizabeth was written, and identification has often been difficult. In some few cases, the most careful search has proved fruitless' (p. xiii). However, she accepts Green's catalogue reference for the Margaret Croft letter.

16 Including Sir George Goring, Sir Dudley Carleton and Sir Constantijn Huygens.

me that in all her time checking Green's calendars against the original State Papers she had never found her to have made a mistake in her cataloguing.[17]

In 1854, remarkably, Green was the first government-appointed external editor of the State Papers housed in the Public Record Office in London. At the time of her appointment she was the author of the highly-acclaimed *Lives of the Princesses of England*, in which she demonstrated her command of archival materials and her mastery of archival skills – including paleography and ancient and modern languages, and a formidable determination to do justice to every fragment of surviving epistolary evidence. It still seems extraordinary today that such a prominent position should have been given to a relatively young woman, and indeed, no other woman held an equivalent position until the twentieth century.[18]

> Over the next forty years Green became the most prolific and among the most highly respected of the editors involved in this monumental government project. When she was approached for the calendars editorship, Green, then aged thirty-six, was editing the diary of John Rous, which was eventually published in 1856. She accepted the appointment, noting her husband's approval, and began work in 1855 at the state paper office. Despite giving birth to a daughter in November 1856, and being assisted in her calendaring work only by her sister Esther Wood, when other editors were provided with staff assistants, Green proved to be the most efficient compiler of calendars, and in 1857 the first volume of *Calendar of State Papers, Domestic, James I* appeared, with its editor identified as Mary Anne Everett Green, 'author of the *Lives of the Princesses of England*'. In the same year she published the *Life and Letters of Henrietta Maria*. She continued at the pace of more than a calendar volume a year for the next thirty-eight years (she edited forty-one volumes in total), while bringing up four children ... Green became a fixture at the Public Record Office, remembered for her indefatigable work habits as well as for feeding pigeons on the steps of the officers' chambers.[19]

17 Dr Katy Mair, personal communication, 9 November 2012.
18 C. L. Krueger, 'Why she lived at the PRO: Mary Anne Everett Green and the profession of history', *The Journal of British Studies* 42 (January, 2003), 65–90. Stable URL: http://www.jstor.org/stable/3594882.
19 Christine L. Krueger, 'Green, Mary Anne Everett (1818–1895)', *Oxford Dictionary of National Biography*, Oxford University Press, 2004; online edn, May 2008, http://www.oxforddnb.com/view/article/11395.

So now I hope you can understand why I was so taken with Green's reference to Margaret Croft's intercepted letter. It had been turned up by the most eminent of State Papers archivists, who had judged it to be of interest (though with some reservations), but who then appeared to have misplaced it.

***

However, the letter Nadine Akkerman and I triumphantly 'found', frankly failed to live up to its promise – or rather, our expectations.

To explain why, I need only quote some of the letter (I can do so almost in its entirety – it is not very long). Here is what our voyage of exploration through the archives in Britain and the Netherlands had eventually uncovered – in my translation from the French:

> Mademoiselle my most dear Cousin
>
> ... I wanted to send you a true account of all the remarkable things that have happened on a tour that the King and Queen, accompanied by the Princess of Orange, have made very recently to North Holland: which I will do in the form of a journal; beginning thus;
>
> Thursday 26th June we left The Hague towards Haarlem in coaches, dressed in our customary travel outfits, with hats in place of bonnets: which caused misunderstanding among the good people who saw us pass; thinking that the Queen and the Princess were young masters William and Lodovick [minor royals], and the rest of us their pages: as also happened to a good woman from Haarlem, who coming to see the Queen, left the room dissatisfied, saying that she had seen three young men at table with no woman in their company. ... We were fortunate enough to find ourselves in Haarlem at the time of the Kermesse carnival which gave us the opportunity to send a large package of presents to The Hague: which arrived opportunely the following day, when Baron Cromwell was entertaining the English Ambassador, and all those of rank from that country at the Court of Holland, so that there was something for everyone: especially Monsieur St Leger; who being interested in pictures received one sent by the Queen: whose subject was a woman angry with her child, beating him so furiously with her hands on his buttocks that his 'juice' [sauce] flowed copiously, all represented in so lively a fashion that the judgement of the spectators was not adequate to know the author: if Monsieur

St Leger (who has a better nose than others in similar matters) had not recognised that it was by the hand of Mabuse [Gossaert].[20]

. . .

Passing through Petten we ate so many mussels, and were served vinegar in place of wine, so that the Countess of Löwenstein was taken with a terrible colic: but as every illness has its remedy, so farting [petter] cured the Petten illness: between which place and Enkhuisen we went through Medemblik, which town being situated at the extreme end of the country, young master William, who met with us there accidentally, having just undertaken a new commission, jumped suddenly out of the Queen's carriage, and throwing himself headlong on the ground to show his humility, kissed the backside of North Holland.

A big fat peasant who acted that day as our guide, taught the company a new refinement by blowing his nose between his fingers, which he wiped by and by on his beard: and having been invited to eat with us as a reward for his good manners, he did not refuse to sit at the top end of the table, nor to be the first to put the hand he had wiped on his beard into every fine dish; most especially into a benefice pie [pasté de benefices] which we thought was reserved for ourselves.

The multi-lingual jokes now get even sharper:

The Cabinet of Doctor Paludanus is the greatest curiosity in Enkhuisen: where among other things worthy of admiration we saw a certain large, thick and stiff instrument: concerning which the Countess of Löwenstein, who understood more than the rest of us about the secrets of nature, desiring to be informed about it asked the Doctor this amiable question: Monsieur Doctor, if you please, What is this Engine. *'Questo è'* (replied the Doctor, who was entertaining us in Italian), *'il valente cazzo d'vn Elephante'* [This is the lusty penis of an Elephant]. I do not understand Italian, replied the Countess. *'Hoc est membrum genitale Elephantis'* [This is the genital member of an Elephant], said the Doctor. Why, say in good French what it is, replied the Countess. The Doctor, finding himself thus hard-pressed, said, 'This is an Elephant's prick to do you good service'.

---

20 Mabuse was the pseudonym of painter Jan Gossaert (1478–1532). This is presumably a joke, since the subject of the painting appears to be scurrilous.

The 29th we reached Hoorn: where the Burgomaster, who was a widower, asked the Queen to give him a wife from among our number; and being allowed to choose he chose the said Countess, but entertained all of us with extravagant compliments: as you may judge from the one he used when greeting the Queen on the morning of our departure, accosting her thus: 'Madam, you have laboured long and hard to get yourself up this morning'.

By the end of the journey the sexual innuendo comes thick and fast:

Arriving [in Amsterdam] on the evening of the first of July, we found Ambassador Carleton with Colonel Morgan awaiting our arrival. . . . We were magnificently received there and paid for (as throughout North Holland) by the local magistrates, and entertained with diverse spectacles: of which the most notable were the two houses of the East and West Indies. In the first we found a banquet of nutmegs, cloves, ginger, and other fruits of the East [Indies]: which encouraged us to go with great zeal to the second, hoping to fill our pockets with gold and silver, as the fruits of the West [Indies]: but that had to wait for the return of the first fleet. In the great scales of the East Indies house the Princess, being weighed against the Queen, was found to have lost several pounds in weight in the four years since they had been in the same place: and on inquiring the reason why from the Sheriff [l'Escoutete]: 'It is because (he said) during that time you have lost your virginity: which is generally a heavy burden for young women.'

. . .

In the evening, thinking to say goodbye to the Magistrates, with the intention of leaving at dawn the following morning for The Hague, the old servant of the Queen who had fallen in love with the Princess [Amalia], kissed her and tickled her with so much affection, playing with his fingers on her buttocks, that the Queen began to be jealous, principally on seeing that the Princess, on the warm insistence of her lover, had agreed to stay one more day in Amsterdam.[21]

So you see, the court circles of the Dutch Stadholder and the Queen of Bohemia really were as full of intrigue and saucy behaviour as that correspondence I came across between Sir Constantijn Huygens and Margaret

21 See full text, Appendix I.

Croft had suggested to me. But unfortunately that does not seem to add much to our understanding of these powerful circles, led by formidable, ambitious, seventeenth-century women. Indeed, its indecorousness makes us uneasy, as it seems to undercut the story scholars have recently begun to tell of how significant as major players on the political stage figures like Elizabeth of Bohemia actually were.[22]

So what are we to do with Croft's letter?

***

I cannot, of course, really end by throwing my hands up in the air and, after all that effort and anticipation, discarding Margaret Croft's intercepted letter – although when I began writing this essay I intended it in part as a cautionary tale to remind us that not everything we scholars undertake in good faith will turn out to yield fruit.[23] Yet after all the effort spent on locating this particular document, transcribing it and translating it in its entertaining detail, surely it can contribute in some way to my continuing scholarly endeavours. So what avenues of research might it open up for us?

Two figures stand from the letter itself – they are the two ladies about whom the scurrilous jokes involving thighs and buttocks are made, Amalia von Solms and the Countess of Löwenstein. At the beginning of 1625, both were maids of honour to Queen Elizabeth of Bohemia. Shortly before the letter was written, Amalia married Frederik Hendrik, the new Dutch Stadholder – almost by accident: Frederik Hendrik was quite a womaniser, Amalia happened to be his latest conquest – and the Countess of Löwenstein replaced her as the leading female member of Elizabeth's household. She served Elizabeth loyally until the Queen's death in 1662. Elizabeth liked to refer to her as 'my merry widow'.[24]

As far as Margaret Croft's letter is concerned, no rules of propriety or decorum separate the behaviour of and towards Amalia von Solms and the Countess of Löwenstein. Amalia is simply the maid of honour

---

22 See Akkerman, *The Correspondence of Elizabeth Stuart*, for example.

23 When I began writing this chapter I was thinking of paying homage to Arlette Farge's *Le goût de l'archive* (Paris: Le Seuil, 1989), which captures brilliantly the archival researcher's emotional investment in the process of excavating meaning from disintegrating documents.

24 Elizabeth Dudley had married the Count of Löwenstein in spring 1622. The marriage occasioned some comment in Elizabeth's correspondence, on the grounds that it was not appropriate for her to retain a married maid of honour. Huygens writes the Countess a letter in May expressing surprise that her new husband has already left to return to the wars. A month later he was dead, and the Countess became a widow. She remained loyally in Elizabeth's service until the Queen of Bohemia's death in 1662.

jumped up into the Stadholder's wife.[25] Yet by the time her husband died in 1647, Amalia had transformed herself into a formidable dowager widow, and her court into one of the European royal centres of opulence and ceremonial.

Which suggests to me that an in-depth study of Amalia von Solms post-1625 would have a great deal to tell us about the extraordinary process of self-conscious elevation which took place in the international reputation of the House of Orange under her astute management.

Personally, though, I really want to know more about the deliciously saucy, intelligent and witty Countess of Löwenstein. When Elizabeth of Bohemia died, in London, having returned to her country of birth after the Restoration to the English throne of her nephew Charles II, the Countess arranged for the Queen's apartments to be sealed (for probate), and took possession of large quantities of goods and jewels in settlement for major sums of money she had loaned Elizabeth in her later years.

But another figure has presided in ghostly form over my lecture – Mary Anne Everett Green, whose tireless efforts cataloguing forty-one volumes of State Papers Domestic in the second half of the nineteenth century made all historians' subsequent research in this period possible. Scholars like myself are bound to acknowledge, sooner or later, that Green is the puppet-mistress who pulls the strings on our excursions into the State Papers. It is her calendars which inevitably guide our searches, and her omissions and elisions, not to mention the compelling running narrative with which she animates the records, which determine where we venture, and where we pass by.

So, since I earlier accused Green of hiding my saucy Margaret Croft letter in The National Archives, let me end with a final telling story which perhaps supports my surmise. I should say that I owe this fitting close to fellow-academic Professor Norma Clarke.[26]

During her long professional life Green moved within a circle of distinguished Victorian men and women of letters. She was one of only three women to sign a public petition in 1851 asking the Public Record Office to offer free access to its records for serious scholars: a request which was granted in 1852. Other signatories included Charles

---

25 I suggest that the tone of Margaret's letter comes directly from the fact that at the time of writing she was amorously entangled with Henry Erskine (see above), and presumably hoped that she too would be catapulted into the aristocracy by a subsequent marriage.

26 Professor Clarke drew my attention to Mary Anne Everett Green's significance for my story during the question period at a 'dry-run' version of this essay which I presented as the plenary lecture at a conference organised by the CELL graduate students.

Dickens, Thomas Babington Macaulay and Thomas Carlyle. One of those to whom Green became particularly close was the influential novelist, writer and reviewer Geraldine Jewsbury – a name to conjure with in her day, but now mostly remembered only for her passionate friendship, extending over a period of more than twenty years, with Thomas Carlyle's wife Jane Welsh Carlyle.

In 1880, during her final illness (she had been diagnosed with inoperable cancer some time earlier), Geraldine turned to State Papers archivist Mary Anne Everett Green for help in putting in order the voluminous body of papers and correspondence she had accumulated during her long and active literary life. Prominent among the items she had treasured over the years was a bundle of intimate letters sent to her by Jane Carlyle.

Jane Carlyle herself had died unexpectedly and suddenly in 1866, leaving her own papers in disorder. When her husband started to put them to rights he discovered, to his distress, that his wife had been deeply unhappy in their relationship, and had confided her unhappiness – with details of what she considered to be unkindness on his part – to many of her literary friends. Stricken with guilt, in 1871 Carlyle passed all Jane's letters to his younger historian colleague and protégé James Anthony Froude, with instructions to publish them as he saw fit after his (Carlyle's) death. The story of the subsequent public scandal is well known to historians of this period.

During his extensive work on the Jane Welsh Carlyle papers Froude naturally consulted Geraldine Jewsbury on a number of occasions. She provided him with a certain amount of detail about her friend's life, which is included in Froude's published volumes. But she apparently withheld the letters (126 of Geraldine's to Jane were among Jane's papers, already in Froude's hands, and were eventually published separately).[27]

Jane and Geraldine's long-running relationship had been an intense one. Early in their correspondence Geraldine had written to Jane Carlyle:

> Oh, my dear, if you and I are drowned, or die, what would become of us if any 'superior person' were to go and write our 'life and

---

27 She appears to be the only friend who told Froude that Thomas Carlyle was impotent, and that this was a major component in Jane's unhappiness. For an 1876 letter to Froude containing Jewsbury's views on Jane Carlyle and her life, see The Carlyle Letters Online, http://carlyleletters.dukejournals.org/cgi/content/full/30/1/ed-30-geraldine-jewsbury-to-froude.

errors'? What a precious mess a 'truthful person' would go and make of us, and how very different to what we really are or were![28]

Shortly before Geraldine Jewsbury's death, on Mary Anne Everett Green's advice, she destroyed the entire bundle of scandalously personal letters from Jane Carlyle.[29] It was, for Green the archival scholar, a matter of propriety, which transcended any responsibilities towards important documents she might feel she had as an archival historian.

The very same women who presided over the painstaking retrieval of the voices of women in the archives for the historical record stood equally vigilant and ready to defend their reputations from the disapproval of posterity. There was a decorum to be observed, in the interests of which even the most scrupulous of archivists might be persuaded to tamper with the evidence.

28 Cit. N. Clarke, *Ambitious Heights: Writing, Friendship, Love – The Jewsbury Sisters, Felicia Hemans and Jane Carlyle* (London: Routledge, 1990), p 15. Apparently, the two women had discussed the fact that they did not wish their correspondence to survive them. Jane's sudden death had prevented her doing any sifting of Geraldine's letters to her.
29 We have this from another woman-friend of the two, in the commentary attached to the published edition of Geraldine's letters to Jane.

2

1688 And All That: Some Curious Consequences of 'Going Dutch'

On 1 November 1688 [new style],[1] driven onward at speed by a strong easterly wind, a vast Dutch fleet left its sheltered harbour at Hellevoetsluis and sailed out into open waters. At a signal from Prince William of Orange the great gathering of ships organised itself into prearranged format, 'stretching the whole fleet in a line, from Dover to Calais, twenty five deep'. The Dutch began their mission, 'colours flying', the fleet 'in its greatest splendour', 'a vast mass of sail stretching as far as the eye could see, the warships on either flank simultaneously thundering their guns in salute as they passed in full view of Dover Castle on one side and the French garrison at Calais on the other'. As the great flotilla proceeded magnificently on its way, the Dutch regiments stood in full parade formation on the deck, 'trumpets and drums playing various tunes to rejoice [their] hearts ... for above three hours'. 'We arrived between Dover and Calais, and at midday, as we passed along the Channel, we could see distinctly the high white cliffs of England, but the coast of France could be seen only faintly.'[2]

These colourful details come from the personal diary (in Dutch) of Constantijn Huygens junior, Prince William's First Secretary, and older brother to Christiaan Huygens, the virtuoso and scientist. Constantijn was at the very forefront of the action throughout the Dutch invasion,

---

1 Throughout the seventeenth century the Julian calendar was followed in England, and the revised Gregorian calendar everywhere else in western Europe. The difference between them was ten days in the seventeenth century and eleven days after 1700 (because England observed 1700 as a leap year, but Continental Europe did not).

2 *Journaal van Constantijn Huygens, den Zoon* 1, 13. Saturday, 13 November: 'Quamen des morgens tusschen Dover en Calis en passeerden smiddaghs het Canael, konnende de hooghe witte Bergen van Engelandt distinctelijck sien, maer de cust van Vranckrijck duysterlijck.'

so it is hardly surprising that other members of his family, back in The Hague, were particularly keenly interested in unfolding events. On 30 December 1688 Christiaan Huygens wrote to Constantijn, expressing his relief at having at last heard that the invasion and military campaign against the forces of James II of England had resulted in a decisive victory:

> It has been extremely upsetting that there has been no way of getting news of you by letter during your long absence, but thank God things will improve from now on. At least the English roads will no longer be blocked.
>
> You may well imagine with what delight we have learned of the great and happy success of affairs there, after all the anxieties and apprehensions since the beginning of this expedition, both because of the dangers at sea and the uncertain prospect for the war. For even though since your departure the news has always been reasonably good, we continued to anticipate a military engagement as long as the King's [James II's] army remained on its feet. And we could not imagine a reversal as sudden as the one which has taken place since the extremely fortunate retreat, which you did not yet know about when you wrote your last letter to Madame your wife.
>
> Now we wait impatiently for news of your arrival in London, and of the reception they will give to Monsieur the Prince which will no doubt be something marvellous to see. What a joy for the nation and what glory for him, to have been successful in such a noble and bold enterprise. We will learn after that how everything is to be established and organised, both over there and back here, which is not a small thing to wait for. We are not sure whether you will return here or stay there where you are, which causes embarrassment for a certain lady of your acquaintance.[3]

Brother Constantijn was now installed in London in a key administrative position, serving as private secretary to the victorious Prince William, shortly to be proclaimed King William III, joint monarch of England with his wife, Princess Mary Stuart, daughter of the deposed English king. Both Huygens brothers were fluent English-speakers – their father Sir Constantijn Huygens having been a lifelong Anglophile (William III too had had a bilingual upbringing).

---

3 See Appendix II.

The Dutch success was so sudden and dramatic, and caused such a general political stir, that Christiaan announced it might even tempt him to join his brother in England: 'If you stay over there [he wrote], you will see that towards the spring there will be a good many people who will take a trip to England, and perhaps I shall be among them.'[4]

Christiaan's keen interest in life in London – now officially an occupied city, with Dutch soldiers posted on every government building, and with sporadic outbursts of violence, especially against Catholics and their places of worship – is palpable.[5] With vicarious enjoyment he urges his brother to take advantage of his new position to make the acquaintance of the English 'virtuosi' (the scientists associated with the Royal Society) without delay – clearly envying him the opportunity:

> In time you will get to know the most eminent men in London and those who understand our great Art [of lens-grinding and telescope-making]. A Mr. Smethwick once sent me some of his lenses (which were however only ocular ones) and claimed that he knew better how to make them than many others. I think that the Royal Society is on a long vacation at the moment. However you might have the opportunity of seeing Mr. Boyle and others of the members.

But he reserves his greatest admiration for Isaac Newton, with whom he has been in correspondence:

> I would love to be in Oxford [actually Cambridge], just to get to know Mr. Newton. I greatly admire the beautiful inventions I find in the work he sent me. I could send you a letter for him, which you might easily find an opportunity to deliver to him.[6]

---

4 'Si vous restez là, vous verrez que vers le printemps il y aura bien des gens qui iront faire un tour en Angleterre et peut estre je seray du nombre.'

5 For detail of the violence that continued for some time after William's arrival see S. Pincus, *1688: The First Modern Revolution* (New Haven & London: Yale University Press, 2009), chapter 9. Pincus's book unfortunately came out after my own *Going Dutch*, so that I was unable to take advantage of its excellent archival additions to the story of the 1688 Revolution/Invasion.

6 'Avec le temps vous pourrez apprendre a connoitre a Londres les illustres et ceux qui s'entendent a nostre grand Art [of lens-grinding]. Il y avoit un Mr. Smetwick qui m'a une fois envoiè des verres de sa façon (ce n'estoient pourtant que des oculaires) et pretendoit qu'il en scavoit plus que beaucoup d'autres. Je pense que la Soc. Royale fait des grandes vacances presentement. Cependant vous pourrez avoir occasion de voir Mr. Boyle et autres des membres. Je voudrois estre a Oxford, seulement pour faire connoissance avec Mr. Newton de qui j'admire extremement les belles inventions que je trouve dans l'ouvrage qu'il m'a envoyè. Je pourray vous envoier une lettre pour luy, que vous trouverez facilement

By February 1689, Christiaan was receiving vivid accounts from scientific acquaintances of the high level of intellectual excitement in London, and was increasingly envious of his older brother's good fortune in being part of unfolding events. Meanwhile, The Hague was rapidly emptying of influential political figures and intellectuals, crossing the Narrow Sea to England as the political centre of gravity shifted to London with the Orange faction.

On 5 February, on the eve of Princess Mary's departure from the Netherlands to join her husband in England for the joint Coronation, Christiaan wrote again to Constantijn. He had heard that his brother might decide not to remain in the service of William (which would necessitate continued residence in England), but rather to return to the Netherlands. Christiaan counselled him to be cautious before taking this course of action, since there were likely to be few jobs back home for the foreseeable future. Here too, as in several other letters, he expresses the view that the English stood to gain far more than the Dutch from the invasion:

> Madame the Princess [Mary] will leave here in 2 days so they say, as long as the wind is favourable, and one can see now by the number of the best houses which are to let and by the decline in rents in general, how deserted The Hague will be. In the end it will only be England who will profit from this great revolution, and the only advantage we here will derive from it is, I think, that without it we would have fallen upon worse times still.[7]

On 15 March, writing this time to his younger brother Lodewijk in Rotterdam, Christiaan reported that Constantijn now looked likely to stay in London, and he once again affirmed his own intention of joining him:

> It seems from his last letters that he no longer shows a desire to quit, that his British Majesty [William] treats him very well, as if planning to retain him. . . . As for myself, I have often wondered whether in such a case I might not obtain a position to improve

moyen de luy faire tenir.' 'A Hofwijck ce 30 Dec. 1688' (Christiaan Huygens, *Oeuvres complètes* (La Haye: M. Nijhoff, 1888–1950), 22 vols: 9, 304–5).

7 'Madame la Princess va partir dans 2 jours a ce qu'on dit pourveu que le vent serve, et l'on voit des a cet heure, combien la Haye sera deserte par la quantitè des meilleures maisons qui sont a louer et par le rabais du louage de toutes en general. Il n'y a que l'Angleterre enfin qui profitera de cette grande revolution et tout l'avantage que nos en tirerons c'est, comme je crois, que sans cela nous serions tombè dans de plus grands malheurs.' (Huygens, *Oeuvres Complètes* 9, 309).

my own fortune, and I had already planned to cross the sea for that purpose. But brother Zulichem [Constantijn] has written to his wife that in 6 weeks (of which 3 are already past) His Majesty might make a triumphant tour of this country, for which reason I have deferred my trip.[8]

'It is a shame', Christiaan added presciently, 'that the Prince has so little love of the study of the sciences. Were this not the case, I should have higher hopes [myself].'

In May, again writing to Lodewijk, Christiaan once more makes it clear that if Constantijn would make up his mind to accept a post with the new Anglo-Dutch régime he too would like an English appointment:

> If [Constantijn] were to have stayed [in England], I could have resolved to transplant myself there also, by obtaining some benefice or pension through his influence, or that of my other friends. . . . [As it is] I can avoid the pain and expense of such a journey. Anyway, I am still undecided.[9]

After Christiaan returned from the trip which, as we shall see, he did finally make to England shortly thereafter, he pressed his older brother with increasing insistence to support his efforts to gain a significant administrative office with William III. He now had other than intellectual motives. In addition to his desire to be where the political and intellectual action was, he found himself financially embarrassed by the high level of taxation being levied in the Netherlands, to support the English invasion and its aftermath:

> I hope that you will give me your assistance in this affair, which is the first with which I have ever troubled you. I would not harbour ambitions like this if I did not believe that it is impossible for me to subsist honestly with the little I have, in this period of exacting taxation, of which there is no end in sight.
>
> For the rest, this post is honourable and not very demanding, which would mean I did not have to give up my other studies. I do not believe that anyone will doubt that I am able to carry out its duties. I beg you therefore not to lose this opportunity to put me a little more at my ease, for in truth I can see nothing in this

8 Huygens, *Oeuvres Complètes* 9, 311; Appendix II.
9 Christiaan to Lodewijk, 14 May 1689. Huygens, *Oeuvres Complètes* 9, 317–18; Appendix II.

country which is suitable for me except one of the places on the Royal Council.[10]

***

These intimate and candid exchanges between members of the Huygens family suggest a rather different set of motives for the visit Christiaan eventually made to London, from June to August 1689, from those conventionally given in Histories of Science. I have myself previously described this trip in terms of Christiaan's having been briefly 'tempted out of retirement'. From my recent closer scrutiny of these and other letters to his brothers it looks rather as if Christiaan harboured serious hopes of rekindling his public career (which had ended in Paris with the death of his patron Colbert in 1685, and the revoking of his right to his French royal pension).

He had domestic reasons for wanting to relocate and revive his public career, too. Following the death of their father Sir Constantijn, eighteen months earlier (on 28 March 1687), Christiaan had been forced to vacate the family home in Het Plein at The Hague (left, as tradition decreed, to Constantijn junior as the new Heer van Zulichem), and to take up residence in the country property at Voorburg, which belonged to the brothers together.[11] He was soon regretting the isolation: 'I have so far stayed at Hofwijck and intend to remain here for the whole winter. There are unpleasant evenings when the weather is bad, but I suppose one can get used to anything', he wrote to Constantijn.[12] He took to staying in the family house in The Hague during the winter months.

Finally – and this is much closer to the traditional background account of his 1689 prolonged stay in London – Christiaan makes it

10 Finally, in late December he writes: 'A la Haye, 23 Dec. 1689. Je ne vous dis plus rien touchant ma sollicitation ne voyant pas qu'il y ait rien a faire tant que S. M.è sera d'avis de ne point remplir la place vacante. . . . Quelque chose de cette nature seroit bien mon fait, et je l'aimerois autant en Angleterre qu'icy, si vous estiez pour y rester, de quoy je commence a douter croiant que peut estre vous accoutumeriez a cette maniere de vie. Je suis logè a la Haye depuis 5 semaines au Noordende, derriere la maison de Mr. van Buttinghe, un peu etroitement mais assez bien au reste. J'ay preferè cela a la solitude trop melancholique de Hofwijck au milieu de l'hyver. J'ai presque achevè l'edition des Traitez de la Lumière et de la Pesanteur dont je vous envoieray des exemplaires' (Huygens, *Oeuvres Complètes* 9, 353).

11 See C. D. Andriesse, *Huygens: The Man Behind the Principle* (Cambridge, Cambridge University Press, 2005), translated S. Miedema (new edition with references and bibliography), p. 351.

12 Huygens, *Oeuvres Complètes* 9, 305: 'Je suis demeurè jusqu'icy à Hofwijc et pretens d'y rester pendant tout l'hyver. Il y a quelque soirees facheuses, quand il fait mauvais temps, mais je vois qu'on s'accoutume a tout.' Eventually he would rent rooms in The Hague for the winter months.

clear in his letters to Constantijn that he is anxious to take advantage of his residence in England to reconnect with old scientific friends. Shortly before the Coronation he wrote:

> I informed you in one of my previous letters that I had the intention of coming to see you, and perhaps I will execute that plan shortly. Not in order to attend the Coronation, but to see some old friends, as well as those who have settled there recently, and to see what they are doing in the way of science, in London, Oxford and Cambridge, in all of which I am quite well known. Here, since your departure, there is not a single person I can talk to about things of that nature.[13]

Christiaan was anxious to renew his aquaintaince with Robert Boyle. But it was above all Sir Isaac Newton whom Christiaan Huygens now badly wanted to meet. For two years he had been working through sections of Newton's *Principia,* of which the author had sent him a presentation copy. Christiaan had engaged with the dense mathematical calculations and bold theorems contained in the *Principia*, with increasing excitement and admiration, even where he disagreed with the Englishman's approach or outcomes.[14]

We have already noted Christiaan telling Constantijn of his enormous admiration for the *Principia*: 'I greatly admire the beautiful inventions I find in the work he sent me.'[15] Fatio de Duillier had seen to it that Christiaan was full of eager anticipation before ever his copy arrived, providing him with a synopsis of its contents while it was still

---

13 22 March 1689. 'Je vous ay mandè par une de mes precedentes que j'avois quelque dessein de vous aller voir, et peut estre je l'executeray dans peu; non pas pour estre spectateur du couronnement, mais pour voir quelques anciens amis, outre ceux qui sont passez nouvellement, et ce qu'on fait en matiere de sciences, tant a Londres qu'a Oxfort et Cambrig ou partout je suis assez connu. Icy depuis vostre depart, je n'ay pas un seul homme a qui parler touchant des choses de cette nature' (Huygens, *Oeuvres Complètes* 9, 312).

14 See, for example, Huygens, *Oeuvres Complètes* 21, 416–26.

15 See Fatio's 1687 letters alerting Christiaan to the imminent publication of the *Principia*. Huygens, *Oeuvres Complètes* 9, 167–8, N. Fatio de Duillier to Christiaan Huygens, 24 June 1687: 'Je me suis déja trouvé trois fois à la Societé roiale où j'ai entendu proposer tantôt d'assez bonnes choses et tantôt d'assez mediocres. Quelques uns de ces Monsieurs qui la composent sont extremement prévenus en faveur d'un livre/ du Monsr. Newton qui s'imprime prsentement et qui se debitera dans trois semaines d'ici. Il m'ont reproché que j'étois trop Cartesien et m'ont fait entendre que depuis les meditations de leur auteur toute la Physique étoit bien changée. Il traite en general de la Mechanique des Cieux; de la maniere dont les mouvemens circulaire qui se font dans un milieu liquide se communique à tout le milieu; de la pesanteur et d'une force qu'il suppose dans toute les planetes pour s'attirer les unes les autres.' 'Mr. Newton de qui j'admire extremement les belles inventions que je trouve dans l'ouvrage qu'il m'a envoyè' (Huygens, *Oeuvres Complètes* 9, 305).

in proof with the Royal Society. 'Let us get hold of Newton's book!' he exclaimed impatiently in a letter to Fatio in July 1687.[16]

As a respected continental virtuoso, Christiaan, once he had got his hands on the *Principia* and read it attentively, had made his high opinion of it widely known. When John Locke came to visit him at Hofwijck, and asked him if he thought the mathematics were sound – Locke admitted he could not himself follow them – Christiaan told him emphatically that they could certainly be trusted. Newton, to whom Locke recounted this, proudly repeated the Dutch mathematician's endorsement in London. A visit to London would at last allow Huygens to meet Newton face to face. More importantly, since Newton's irascible nature was legendary, the great man would be predisposed to enter into debate with the Dutchman, who was so publicly enthusiastic about his work.

***

The Prince of Orange arrived in England in November 1688 with a formidable army. But he also came prepared for his encounter with the English, with a fully formed outlook and set of attitudes. A robust set of common interests and commitments had developed over at least the preceding half-century between a certain sort of Englishman and his Dutch counterpart. While there was always an edge of suspicion (there had, after all, been three Anglo–Dutch wars since the 1650s), there was also a great deal of recognisably shared experience, particularly in the realm of arts and letters.

A small episode on the road leading from Torbay to London and the English throne underlines the importance of this shared 'mentality'. Constantijn Huygens junior records in his diary that in the course of the often arduous and demanding forced march from Torbay to London, Prince William of Orange took some time off from military affairs to do a bit of tourism, and encouraged his secretary to do likewise.

On 4 December, as the Prince travelled towards London at the head of his massive Dutch army, he insisted on making a detour to admire Wilton House near Salisbury, the country seat of the Earl of Pembroke. Wilton was renowned for its architecture and its art, but most of all for its magnificent gardens, designed in the 1640s by Isaac de Caus.

Engravings of the Wilton gardens had appeared in a lavishly illustrated book entitled *Hortus Pembrochianus* (Garden of the Earl

16 Huygens, *Oeuvres Complètes* 9, 190, Christiaan Huygens to N. Fatio de Duillier, 11 July 1687: 'Mes respects a M. Boyle. Ayons le livre de Newton.'

of Pembroke), first published in 1645–6, and reprinted several times thereafter – in one case, without any of the accompanying text, but simply as a set of engravings. The book is closely modelled on a famous volume brought out twenty-five years earlier by Isaac de Caus's brother Salomon, depicting the fabulous gardens he had designed at Heidelberg for the 'Winter King and Queen' – the Elector Palatine Frederick and his wife, Charles I's sister, Elizabeth of Bohemia. Both books are likely to have been familiar to a keen enthusiast for gardens like Prince William. Heidelberg's gardens had been destroyed during the Thirty Years War, along with the city's great university and its library.

In the midst of a military campaign, on foreign soil, William took the earliest possible opportunity to inspect the Pembroke gardens in all their glory, and at some length. Constantijn Huygens junior records the detour made for this purpose:

> We marched from Hendon to Salisbury, 13 miles, a good way through Salisbury plain, but for a long time we had a cold, sharp wind blowing directly in our faces.

> A mile from Salisbury we passed an undistinguished village (which nevertheless sends two representatives to Parliament), called Wilton, where the Earl of Pembroke has a rather beautiful house which is moderately beautiful, because there are some very notable paintings by Van Dyck. His Highness went to see it, but I did not – I was in a hurry to get to the town to get warm.[17]

William may have been anxious to see the Van Dycks, at least one of which showed his mother as a child, with her siblings, but the gardens were far more impressive than the house. Laid out and planted before the house itself was built, as was customary for the period, the Wilton gardens had been designed to complement a classical villa on a grand scale, as de Caus's original drawings clearly show. By the time the house was constructed, the 4th Earl's fortunes had faded, and a more modest house eventually presided over the parterres and wildernesses, statues and elaborate fountains.

Wilton House's architecture, interior decoration, artworks and gardens were entirely to the monarch-to-be's Dutch taste. The weather was abominable, but that in no way dampened the Stadholder's enthusiasm. Rejoining Huygens the following day, William told

17 *Journaal van Constantijn Huygens, den Zoon* I, 35.

Constantijn that the house and garden were as outstanding as he had been led to believe: 'In the evening the Prince was in his room coughing violently, having caught cold. He told me I absolutely must go and see the house at Wilton.'[18] Huygens 'did want to go to Wilton, but my horses were not available'. He went on foot to see Salisbury Cathedral instead.[19]

So the milieu (what the French call the 'cadre') was familiar to the two Huygens brothers, on both sides of the Channel.

***

So now that we have a context provided by that fascinating exchange of familiar letters, let us reassess what happened on the occasion of the trip that Christiaan Huygens eventually made to England.

Both Huygens brothers kept diaries for this period.[20] So we know Christiaan arrived in Harwich on 1 June 1689 [old style], having travelled from The Hague in the company of Constantijn's wife and young son. They reached London five days later. Constantijn recorded in his diary for 6 June:

> While I was seated at table in Whitehall, my wife, son and brother arrived and, to my great joy, all in good health. In the afternoon we looked over one or two lodgings with them and cousin Becker took one with Mrs Row, widow of Sir Robert Row, and spoke with the daughter. Our rooms, together with those of brother Christiaan, cost 33 guilders per week. We moved in straightaway, after we had been out shopping.[21]

The whole family frequented the court of William and Mary at Hampton Court, where the couple had taken up official residence, because the sea-coal pollution at Whitehall exacerbated William's asthma. So from his arrival Christiaan found himself at the very heart of unfolding political events in England – part of the new, Dutch ruling élite. I might add that his diary reveals that he spent the greater part of his almost three months in England enjoying the kinds of recreational activities – gambling, trips to stately homes, musical entertainment – that you would expect a courtier to engage in.

---

18 'De Prins savants in sijn camer seer hoestende en verkoudt zijnde, seyde mij dat nootsakelijck het huys te Wilton moste gaen sien.'
19 *Journaal van Constantijn Huygens, den Zoon* I, 36.
20 For Christiaan's diary of the visit, see Huygens, *Oeuvres Complètes* 22, 743–9. See also Huygens, *Oeuvres Complètes* 9, 333.
21 Cit. Andriesse, *Huygens*, pp. 356–7.

He visited Wren's new buildings: the nearly completed St Paul's, the Monument to the Great Fire (in fact more Hooke's), the Temple and Bedlam (Bethlehem Hospital, also by Hooke). There were trips to Windsor Castle, where Christiaan admired Verrio's ceiling paintings in St George's Chapel, and outings to take the waters at Epsom and to visit the Evelyn home at Deptford, with its remarkable garden. On a gambling evening at Epsom in the company of Constantijn and his wife, he won a silver ewer worth 10 and a half guineas. He went to the theatre, and to several musical soirées, during one of which he listened to French Opera and an accomplished flautist.

Towards the end of his stay he also embarked on an amorous liaison with a Miss Pernell, the intimate details of which are concealed in Christiaan's diary behind a series of indecipherable coded entries.

It was from this position of relaxed privilege and public prominence, and with the authority of his brother and the court behind him, that on 12 June, shortly after his arrival, Christiaan travelled by boat back along the Thames to Gresham College to attend a meeting of the Royal Society.[22] As he recorded in his diary, this meeting was in strong contrast to the glamour of life at court:

> To Gresham College. Meeting in a small room. Cabinet of curiosities, extensive but poorly maintained. Hoskins presided. Henshaw was one of the principals. Halley. Van Leeuwenhoek's letter delivered. I was accompanied by Mr. Newton and Mr. Fatio.[23]

This diary entry tells us that Christiaan had now met Newton, formally introduced, one imagines, by Fatio de Duillier. Two weeks later, having returned to Hampton Court, Christiaan Huygens's diary records that he had an audience with King William and dined with the king's Dutch favourite, William Bentinck, now Earl of Portland, the most powerful man at court. It had been suggested beforehand that, as an esteemed virtuoso particularly well-connected with the Dutch royal household, Christiaan might intervene with William III on Isaac Newton's behalf, putting the mathematician's name forward for a promotion.

---

22 On 10 [20] June, according to Constantijn's diary, Christiaan visited Robert Boyle (cit. Andriesse, *Huygens*, p. 357).

23 'Gresham Colleg, assemblez dans une petite chamber. Cabinet de raretez, copieux mais peu proprement entretenu. Askin [Hoskins] presidoit. Henschau [Henshaw] un des principaux. Halley. Rendu la lettre de Leeuwenhoek. J'y fus avec Mr. Newton et Mr Fatio' (Huygens, *Oeuvres Complètes* 22, 744).

Two days later, according to Constantijn's diary, Christiaan acted directly on Newton's behalf a second time – once again, the Dutch faction intervening decisively in the lives of English subjects:

> 10 July. Brother Christiaan went to London with young Mr. Hambden, Fatio de Duillier and Mr. Newton at 7 in the morning with the purpose of recommending Mr. Newton to the King for a vacancy as Head of a Cambridge College.[24]

On 28 July, Christiaan attended a fashionable concert, at which Hampden introduced him to the Duke of Somerset, Chancellor of the University of Cambridge, and Newton's preferment was once more discussed:

> To Hampton Court to speak to the King. Dined with Mr. Bentinck, Count of Portland. Slept at Dutton. Mr. Haden presented me, and invoked my expertise [m'avoit alleguè] in favour of Mr. Newton, on whose behalf he was importuning His Majesty.[25]

Here, the diaries of both brothers record, Christiaan Huygens was engaged in serious, not to say significant business. He was prominently and personally involved in the political game of snakes-and-ladders as a result of which Isaac Newton – hitherto a reclusive intellectual and a comparatively minor figure, politically – moved centre-stage. His brother Constantijn's diary confirms the importance that was attached to this intervention of Christiaan's.

The Cambridge college whose headship Newton had ambitions to fill was King's, and the court lobbyist on Newton's behalf, who approached Huygens, was John Hampden, a leading Parliamentary player. Huygens's approach evidently had the desired effect. Shortly thereafter, William III wrote to the Fellows of King's College, informing them of his desire that they appoint Newton as their new Provost. There

---

24 'Quoiqu'ayant parlé deux fois dans son Journal de la sollicitation de Newton, il n'a pas noté ce que le frère Constantyn écrit dans son Journal à lui: "10 juillet. Frère Christiaen alla avec le jeune Mr. Hambden et Faccio Duillier et Mr. Newton le matin à 7 heures à Londres dans le dessein de recommander ce dernier au Roi pour une place vacante de Régent d'un collège à Cambridge". Il s'agissait du poste de préfect de King's College. Nous avons noté dans le T. XXI qu'à Gresham College, le 22 juin, Huygens parla sur la pesanteur. Nous pouvons ajouter que Newton traita de la double réfraction' (Huygens, *Oeuvres Complètes* 22, 749).

25 'A Hamptoncourt parlè au Roy. Disnè chez Mr. Bentingh Comte de Portland. Couchè a Dutton. Mr. Hamden me presenta et m'avoit alleguè en faveur de Mr. Newton pour qui il sollicitoit Sa Majestè' (Huygens, *Oeuvres Complètes* 22, 744).

was only so far, given university politics, that such influential lobbying could take a candidate. The new foreign king was roundly rebuffed by the Fellows, who chose another candidate. Nevertheless, Newton's public career was clearly in the ascendent, thanks in no small part to the brothers Huygens.[26]

Even though this direct attempt by Christiaan Huygens to advance Newton's career proved unsuccessful, it significantly strengthened the relationship between the two men, and with it the intensity of the intellectual bond between them. In August, before Christiaan returned home, Newton presented him with two papers on motion through a resisting medium, in response to his *Discours de la cause de la Pesanteur*. Autograph copies of these papers (marked 'received in London, August 1690' by Huygens), and Huygens's notes in response, survive. The two men also had lengthy discussions of optics and colour. Huygens told Leibniz that Newton had communicated 'some very beautiful experiments' to him – probably his experiments with thin films similar to the ones Huygens himself had performed twenty years earlier, and similar to those Robert Hooke had recorded in his *Micrographia* even earlier.[27]

In the domain of science and virtuosity, Christiaan did not confine himself to constructing a solid relationship with Newton. In pursuit of his general aim of re-establishing his connections with the London scientific virtuosi, he did indeed see Robert Boyle, and was shown experiments that delighted him in the field of what we would call chemistry, but in the period was actually closer to alchemy:

> Saw Mr Boyle 3 times. On the last occasion he showed us an experiment with two cold liquids which burst into flame when they were combined. He had moistened a piece of wool in a silver spoon with the first, which had a strong smell almost like oil of anis. The other, which was poured on to it, was in a tiny vial, and gave off fumes when the stopper was removed.[28]

---

26 R. S. Westfall, *Never at Rest: A Biography of Isaac Newton* (Cambridge: Cambridge University Press, 1983), p. 480.

27 Westfall, *Never at Rest*, p. 488.

28 'Vu Mr. Boile 3 fois. A la derniere il nous fit voir l'experience de deux liqueurs froides qui estant mises ensemble faisoient une flame. De l'une, qui avoit une senteur forte presque comme de l'huile d'anis, il avoit mouillè de la laine dans une ceuillere d'argent. L'autre qu'on versa dessus estoit dans une tres petite phiole, et fumoit quand on ostoit le couvercle' (Huygens, *Oeuvres Complètes* 22, 746). See also his farewell to Boyle: '19 Aug. Pris congè de Mr Boijle, de Mr. Fatio, et Mr. Locke. De Mr. Witsen et chez Me. P. f. le f. Mr. Boijle me promit la recepte pour faire de la glace sans glace ni neige' (Huygens, *Oeuvres Complètes* 22, 747).
      Boyle finally sent the recipe in April 1690, after several reminders via Constantijn. Huygens, *Oeuvres Complètes* 9, 407; Huygens, *Oeuvres Complètes* 19, 684.

By the beginning of 1689, Newton had already emerged as one of the most prominent Protestant-supporting members of the Cambridge University community, with impeccable credentials to serve the incoming regime. On 15 January he had been elected one of the three University representatives to the national Convention appointed to settle the legitimacy of William and Mary's claim to the English throne. He came to London to sit on the Convention, and remained there until early the next year. Following the Coronation of William and Mary, the Convention to which he had been appointed became the Convention Parliament, and Newton remained in the capital until a week after it was prorogued on 27 January 1690.

Nevertheless, Christiaan Huygens's intervention with the new Dutch king was of no small importance to Newton. It surely helped ensure, when the two of them went together to that meeting of the Royal Society on 12 June (much reported and commented on in the History of Science literature) that it was Huygens's contributions on gravity and light to which Newton attended seriously. I have written elsewhere about the way in which, on that same occasion, he and the other Royal Society Fellows who were present ignored Robert Hooke's contributions on these topics – Hooke, predictably, took grave offence.[29]

We tend to be told that Christiaan Huygens retreated to his self-imposed life as an intellectual invalid on his return to The Hague. In fact, as we have seen, he made serious – not to say energetic – efforts to re-enter mainstream social life, and to revive his international scientific activities. He eventually moved from Hofwijck to rented rooms in Nordeinde because Hofwijck was too cut off from civilised conversation. He wrote repeatedly to Constantijn urging him to intervene on his behalf to obtain a position at the court of William and Mary that had recently fallen vacant. He rebuilt his scientific and intellectual links with key members of the Royal Society, particularly with Newton and Robert Boyle.

If he was unsuccessful in procuring that administrative post with the new King William, it was not for want of his – or his brother's – efforts. Constantijn approached the new king on at least two occasions to press Christiaan's suit for the vacant place on his Council. In the end, Constantijn records in his diary that, just as Christiaan feared, William's lack of interest in science prevented him from valuing any possible

29   See L. Jardine, *Going Dutch: How England Plundered Holland's Glory* (London: HarperCollins, 2008).

contribution he would be able to make on his behalf, and to conclude that Christiaan was overqualified for an administrative post:

> Following a second letter, in which brother Christaan tormented me to ask the King for a place in his Council, vacant since Pettecum's death, I spoke to him about it, and he told me through clenched teeth that he was not sure he would fill that vacancy. When, shortly afterwards, I told him again that he would be well served by my brother, who is of a penetrating intelligence and applies himself assiduously to everything he does, he replied that he thought that my brother had ideas which were too high-minded for him to dawdle (or some such word) with the administrators, so I did not insist any further.[30]

From the point of view of a possible shared Anglo-Dutch intellectual tradition, what an irony it now seems, that the deposed English Catholic king James II should have been passionate about the new science, while the Dutch Protestant William III was utterly indifferent to it.

How different might it have been – how much more conclusively a shared tradition – had Christiaan obtained that post in William III's Council, for which he pressured his influential brother in letter after letter in late 1689 and early 1690. One can only speculate about how fruitful might have been the collaborative deliberations between Christiaan Huygens and Sir Isaac Newton if they had only been in a position to sit down together, on a regular basis, in some comfortable drawing room at Whitehall or Hampton Court in the years following the 'Glorious Revolution'.

---

30 Cit. Huygens, *Oeuvres Complètes* 9, 336, note 1 to letter of 9 September 1689: 'A l'occasion de cette lettre, Constantyn, frère, nota encore dans son journal, le 25 septembre: "Sur une seconde lettre, avec laquelle frère Christiaan me tourmenta pour demander au Roi la place dans son conseil, vacante par la mort de Pettecum, je lui en parlai et il dit entre ses dents qu'il ne savait pas s'il remplirait cette place. Lorsque, peu après, je disais encore, que je croyais qu'il ne serait pas mal servi par mon frère, comme étant d'une intelligence pénétrante et de bonne application il répondit, qu'il croyait qu'il avait des idées plus hautes que de s'attarder (ou quelque mot pareil) avec les administrateurs, sur quoi je n'insistais plus".'

3

Never Trust a Pirate: Christiaan Huygens's Longitude Clocks

On 13/23 January 1665[1] Sir Robert Moray, courtier and confidant to King Charles II, and sometime President of the Royal Society in London, wrote to the talented young mathematician and horologist Christiaan Huygens at The Hague:

> At last Captain Holmes has returned, and the account he has given us of the experiment with the pendulum clocks leaves us in absolutely no doubt as to their success.

> He left the island of Saint Thomas, which is under the Line, accompanied by four vessels. In order to pick up the correct wind for his return he was obliged to steer towards the West and to sail for six hundred leagues without changing his course, after which, finding a favourable wind, he steered towards the coast of Africa, heading directly North North-East. But when he had sailed four or five hundred leagues in this direction, the Masters of the three ships under his command, fearing that they would run out of water before they reached their pretended destination, proposed that they should steer a course towards Barbados. In pursuit of which the Captain, having brought them all together with their Journals [log books] they were found to be at odds with the calculations of the Captain, one by 80 leagues, the other by 100 and the third by 120. For the Captain calculated using his pendulum clocks that he was hardly more than 30 leagues away from the

---

1 Throughout the seventeenth century the Julian calendar was followed in England, and the revised Gregorian calendar everywhere else in western Europe. The difference between them was ten days in the seventeenth century and eleven days after 1700 (because England observed 1700 as a leap year, but Continental Europe did not).

Island of Fuego, which is one of the islands of Cape Verde, from which the three Pilots estimated that they were still at a considerable distance. And because the Captain had total confidence in the clocks, he insisted that they continue in his proposed route, and the following morning the Island of Fuego appeared just as he has judged would happen.[2]

Christiaan Huygens was the man who patented that great breakthrough in accurate timekeeping, the pendulum clock, in 1657. For over a year he had been awaiting the outcome of a series of sea-trials of his clocks, to establish whether they might keep time with sufficient precision to allow an horological solution to the calculation of longitude. These had been undertaken by Robert Holmes on a voyage to the Guinea Coast of Africa sponsored by the Royal African Company.[3] Huygens had written repeatedly to Moray for news of the trials, hence that 'At last' at the beginning of Moray's letter.

On 5 February Huygens wrote to a close friend, Jean Chapelain, to tell him of his successful application to the States General for a Dutch patent for his longitude clock, based on Holmes's testimony.

On his return, Captain Holmes has lodged his report concerning the usefulness of pendulum clocks, which goes far beyond my expectations. I could never have imagined that clocks of this first, preliminary mode of construction could have succeeded so well, and I had reserved my principal hopes for the new ones. But since these have already been so successful, and that the others are even more precise, I feel entitled to believe that the discovery of true longitude will shortly reach its final perfection. . . . The pendulum clocks are a success. The Estates General want to see the clock at their Assembly.[4]

Moray's account of Holmes's remarkable success with the pendulum clocks was published immediately, almost verbatim, in the Royal Society's *Philosophical Transactions* and in French in the *Journal des sçavans*, together with extracts of his letter to Chapelain. I say almost verbatim, because at several points in the narrative phrases have been

2 Christiaan Huygens, *Oeuvres complètes* (La Haye: M. Nijhoff, 1888–1950), 22 vols: 5, 204.
3 For the sponsorship letter, see *Captain Robert Holmes his Journalls of Two Voyages into Guynea in his M[ajestie]s Ships the Henrietta and the Jersey*, Pepys Library Sea MSS No. 2698, pp. 175–7.
4 *Journal des sçavans* (1665), pp. 95–6. Summary. Huygens, *Oeuvres Complètes* 5, 222–3.

inserted: 'having there adjusted his Watches', 'having a great confidence in the said Watches'.[5]

The same account translated into Dutch eventually featured as the unique account of a sea-trial of pendulum clocks to be included in Huygens's landmark book on pendulum clocks, the *Horologium Oscillatorium*, published in 1673. It formed the basis for Huygens's determined efforts to secure a patent for his 'longitude clock' in Holland, France and England.

Right down to the present day, it is the spectacular success of these trials which is invoked as the crucial evidence, on the basis of which Huygens's pendulum-clock timekeepers take their place as a significant step along the path from the theoretical aspiration to determine longitude at sea using a precision clock, to the realisation of that dream with John Harrison's longitude timekeeper.

The problem is that Sir Robert Holmes (as he later became) was not known as a person of integrity. Quite the contrary: Major Robert Holmes, as he was at the time of the Guinea sea-trials, was somewhat notorious, as a notable villain. Or at least, he is infamous as the hot-tempered, violent and uncontrollable naval commander whose unprovoked attacks on Dutch shipping and seizure of Dutch goods were directly responsible for starting both the second and third Anglo-Dutch wars.[6]

Holmes had served under Prince Rupert and James, Duke of York, and eventually rose to the rank of Admiral. In 1664, on the very voyage on which he was ostensibly testing the Huygens clocks,[7] he sacked the Dutch trading-stations along the coast of Guinea one by one, seizing goods and property and laying waste the Dutch settlements. On his return he was twice imprisoned in the Tower of London (on 9 January and 14 February 1665), for having gone beyond orders or for failing to bring back adequate amounts of booty (it is not quite clear which). His actions led directly to the Dutch declaring war on 22 February 1665 (by

---

5 *Philosophical Transactions of the Royal Society* 1(1665–6), 13–15.

6 On Holmes's naval career, see R. Ollard, *Man of War: Sir Robert Holmes and the Restoration Navy* (London: Hodder & Stoughton, 1969). Ollard also makes use of Holmes's Journal in the Pepys Library, but only as a biographical source.

7 More accurately, the 'Bruce–Huygens' clocks. Alexander Bruce, second earl of Kincardine, married the daughter of the Dutch nobleman Cornelius van Aerssen, Baron Somelsdyk, and throughout the English Commonwealth period was Christiaan Huygens's neighbour in The Hague. For a number of years they worked on pendulum-clock development together. The clocks Holmes tested were jointly developed by the two of them. See M. Mahoney, 'Christian Huygens: The measurement of time and of longitude at sea', in H. J. M. Bos et al. (eds), *Studies on Christiaan Huygens* (Lisse: Swets, 1980), pp. 234–270.

announcing that they would retaliate against any British shipping in the Guinea region), at which point Holmes was released and pardoned, in order to command His Majesty's forces.

In August 1666, Holmes attacked and destroyed by fire 150 East Indiamen in the Vlie estuary and sacked the town of Westerschelling on adjacent Terschelling Island. In 1672, Holmes and Sir Frescheville Holles attacked the Dutch East India Company convoy returning from Smyrna in the English Channel, seizing its cargo of salt and Oriental luxuries, thereby precipitating the third Anglo-Dutch war of that year.

Samuel Pepys was afraid of Holmes ('an idle, proud, conceited, though stout fellow'), and on several occasions expressed reluctance at having to deal with him on matters of naval discipline. After the second Dutch war Holmes was rewarded for his exploits with the Governorship of the Isle of Wight; he eventually became extremely rich and much more respectable.[8]

It was Huygens himself who first smelled a rat regarding Holmes's report of the spectacularly successful performance of the 'pendula'. On 6 February 1665 (the day after his upbeat letter to his friend Chapelain), in his first response to Moray, Huygens, after expressing his delight at the dramatic outcome of the trials, added a small caveat:

> I have to confess that I had not expected such a spectacular result from these clocks. To give me ultimate satisfaction, I beg you to tell me what you and your colleagues at the Royal Society think of this Relation [of Holmes's], and if the said Captain seems a sincere man whom one can absolutely trust. For it must be said that I am amazed that the clocks were sufficiently accurate to allow him by their means to find such a tiny island [as Fuego].[9]

On 6 March, Huygens was still pressing Moray for 'something of the detail of what you have learned from Mr Holmes, principally in order to

---

8 It is via the Isle of Wight route that Holmes's path crossed that of Robert Hooke (born on that island). It has been plausibly argued that Grace, Robert Hooke's niece, was the mother of Holmes's illegitimate daughter Mary. See L. Jardine, *The Curious Life of Robert Hooke: The Man Who Measured London* (London: HarperCollins, 2003).

9 Huygens, *Oeuvres Complètes* 5, 224. Huygens's attitude to his first longitude clocks was entirely consistent: he doubted their suitability from the start. While still waiting for Bruce finally to set off for England on the first trials in 1662 he wrote to his brother telling him that the clocks Bruce was taking with him were not performing as well as he hoped, and cautioning him not to talk them up until he (Huygens) had conducted further tests on 'the clock I have now ordered' whose design he trusted more (*Oeuvres Complètes* 4, 285).

know how the clocks behaved in a storm, and if in that climate rust did not eventually cause them to stop'.[10]

The matter of Holmes's trustworthiness was raised at the 8 March meeting of the Royal Society (at which Huygens's concerns were raised, and the letter of 6 March read):

> It was affirmed by several of the members, that there was an error in [Holmes's] relation, as to the island named therein; and that it was not the island of Fuego, which the Major's ships had touched in order to water there, but another thirty leagues [90 nautical miles] distant from it.[11]

Samuel Pepys (recently elected a Fellow) was 'desired to visit the Major, and to inquire farther concerning this particular for the satisfaction of the society'. In practice this meant visiting Holmes in the Tower, where he was still imprisoned for his conduct towards the Dutch settlements at Guinea, during his voyage.[12] On 14 March Pepys attended 'a farewell dinner which [Sir John Robinson, Lieutenant of the Tower] gives Major Holmes at his going out of the Tower', 'Here a great deal of good victuals and company'.[13]

On 3/13 March Moray responded again to Huygens's pressing him for further detail from Holmes. He still had no concrete data from Holmes, but on the basis of conversations with one of his sea captains, he himself volunteered some significant corrections to the original account given:

> I am due to dine with Mr Holmes tomorrow, and it is my intention to try to get his account in writing, which he promised me when

10 Huygens, *Oeuvres Complètes* 5, 256. Moray's responses were both reassuring and evasive. 'I have not seen Captain Holmes since he told me the story of his Clocks. But he has repeated the same thing since to My Lord Brouncker (he was then prisoner in the Tower). He has now been freed, but I do not know where he lodges. As soon as we meet I expect to have from him in writing everything further he is able to say further about these Clocks. . . . For the rest I have no doubt as to the truthfulness of Holmes. Still, since in giving me his account of the experiment he made he referred to the Captains and Masters of the three other vessels which were with him, I expect to learn from them as soon as I can, if everything happened as he has recounted it to us' (Huygens, *Oeuvres Complètes* 5, 234).

11 T. Birch, *The history of the Royal Society of London for improving of natural knowledge, from its first rise, in which the most considerable of those papers communicated to the Society, which have hitherto not been published, are inserted as a supplement to the Philosophical transactions*, 4 volumes (London: A. Millar, 1756–1757): 2, 21.

12 For a clear sense of the concern caused by Holmes's conduct on that voyage, and Pepys's lack of trust of him, see *The Diary of Samuel Pepys*, 11 volumes (London: HarperCollins, 1995): 6, 43.

13 Pepys, *Diary* 6, 56.

we last parted. However, I have spoken to another officer of one of the ships which were with him, who was himself on the Major's ship until they reached the island of Saint Thomas, and is indeed the person who had care of the Clocks, and from whom we had the first report on them 14 or 15 months ago [during an earlier voyage].[14]

'I do not blame [Major Holmes] for this', he insists. But again, 'There remains one further objection that I know of which reduces the accuracy of this experiment, which is the precise location of the Island of Fuego [which Holmes has miscalculated]' – not exactly a ringing endorsement of Holmes's story.

On 15 March, both Pepys and Moray reported to the Royal Society on their dealings with Holmes. Pepys had spoken to the master of 'the Jersey ship' – that is, Holmes's own vessel.

> The said master affirmed, that the vulgar reckoning proved as near as that of the watches, which [the clocks], added he, had varied from one another unequally, sometimes backward, sometimes forward, to 4, 6, 7, 3, 5 minutes; as also that they had been corrected by the usual account. And as to the island, at which they had watered, the said master declared, that it was not Fuego, but another 30 miles distant from the same westward.[15]

According to the Master of Holmes's ship, then, there was not much to choose between the old way of calculating longitude, and that using the new clocks. Moray, who had spoken to Holmes himself, corrected 'some mistakes in the number of the leagues formerly mentioned' (informed of these errors, Huygens expressed the hope that they would be corrected in any future edition of works on longitude clocks which included this important testimony – and indeed, the figures in the printed versions of Holmes's story have been altered from those in Moray's original letter to Huygens). Holmes's Master also confirmed that the ships had not watered on Fuego, 'yet they had made that island at the time, which the Major had foretold, and were gone from thence to another, more convenient, for watering'.[16]

---

14 Huygens, *Oeuvres Complètes* 5, 269–71.
15 Birch, *The history of the Royal Society* 2, 23.
16 Moray also added two further experiments Holmes claimed to have carried out with the clocks. Birch, *The history of the Royal Society* 2, 23.

At the very next meeting of the Royal Society, on 22 March, 'Mr Pepys was desired to procure the journals of those masters of ships, who had been with Major Holmes in Guinea, and differed from him in the relation concerning the pendulum watches.'[17] Nothing further was heard, however, of discrepancies between the ship's journals and his 'relation concerning the pendulum clocks'. Had that convivial dinner a week earlier perhaps predisposed Pepys to draw a veil over the matter? In any case, by this time England was at war with Holland, and Holmes himself was in charge of English naval hostilities.

Holmes's account of his trials of Huygens's longitude clocks has been firmly lodged on the record ever since, as an exact account of the astonishing success of these critical sea-trials of Huygens's pendulum clocks.

However, a presentation copy of Holmes's journal of his two Guinea voyages survives in the Pepys Library at Magdalene College, Cambridge. It is presumably the copy Pepys procured, as instructed by the Royal Society, to validate Holmes's narrative. It has gone unnoticed by scholars, in the context of the Holmes trials of Huygens's longitude clocks on that very voyage.[18]

Holmes's journal is extremely full and specific. It is also rather well written – Holmes has a nice line in racy narratives, particularly where bombarding and plundering Dutch merchant ships is concerned. Day by day he chronicles the progress of his band of ships – the *Jersey*, the *Brill*, the *Golden Lyon* and the *Expedition*. Only once in the course of the entire journal does he mention the pendulum clocks, and it is hard to see how they could have been kept going steadily, given a series of buccaneering adventures and naval battles with Dutch East Indiamen in which (for instance) Holmes's topmast and mainsail were shot away.

Here is a taste of Holmes's swashbuckling style, and a reminder of the combative nature of his maritime ventures, as preserved in a letter he included in his Guinea voyages journals written from Lisbon on his return journey:

17 Birch, *The history of the Royal Society* 2, 26.
18 I owe this discovery to some chance remarks in C. H. Wilson, 'Who captured New Amsterdam?', *The English Historical Review*, 72 (1957), 469–74: 'Fortunately our answer [to the question of whether Holmes was involved in the capture of New Amsterdam in 1664] need not rest on surmise, for we have Holmes's own account of his movements during the months when he is supposed by some historians to have been on his way to America, and capturing New Amsterdam [*Captain Robert Holmes his Journalls of Two Voyages into Guynea in his Mts Ships The Henrietta and the Jersey*, Pepys Library Sea MSS. No. 2698]' (pp. 472–3).

Since my Letters from Cape Coast wee have taken in Aga & Anamaboa the former by storm, and after promiseing Quarter to the Flemins & taken possession our men being somewhat greedy of Plunder, the Flemins treacherously blew up the Powder & withall 80 or 90 whites and Blacks which the Blacks rewarded by cutting of all their heads; At my Return from the Coast all things were in a good Posture, & well settled. I haue with me here the Golden Lyon, the Crown and Brill which I hope to man here & carry them for Engl[an]d. I know not how my Actions vpon the Coast of Guyny are resented at Court, nor how my Condicon stands.[19]

So what does Holmes's journal tell us about the 'experiment' he conducted with Huygens's timekeepers?

In July 1664, Holmes was on San Thome, reprovisioning and rewatering. He set out for home on 11 August. For more than a month strong currents, contrary winds and becalmings bedevilled him. By the third week of September they were well and truly lost on the open seas.[20] There is indeed a full sequence of entries relating to Holmes and his fellow captains getting lost and running short of water, which does, uniquely in the entire journal, mention 'pendula' (this fair copy of the journal was prepared for James, Duke of York, the future James II). It was with great reluctance that Holmes's companions agreed to turn eastwards. It was three days before they sighted land, during which time variable winds took them in several different directions. As Pepys had learned, they did not land on Fuego, but some time later on another of the Cape Verde Islands, St Vincent. In the matter of the accuracy with which the 'pendula' enabled Holmes accurately to predict his eastwards landfall, he had, at the very least, greatly exaggerated.

But once Holmes's misleading report, with its bravura claims for the pendulum clocks, was on the record in England, France and Holland, and publicly unchallenged, Huygens's claim to priority in relation to

19 The letter begins: 'Captain Holmes to Mr Coventry. Jearzy Lisbon 9 Nov. 1664. Sir, Meeting on Sunday last off Lisbon Barr rdg a Dartmouth vessell bound home, I writt by her to you to let you know of my arrivall here after a long & tedious passage occasioned by contrary winds, calms & foule weather, & lest my letter should miscarry I tooke the opportunity of writeing to you by this Ship; My Main Mast, Bouspritt & Mainyard being defective I was forced in here to be supplyed & to refit the other Ships with me, not able to keep the Sea: As soon as I haue finished, I will make the best of my way for England' (*Captain Robert Holmes his Journalls of Two Voyages*, p. 168).

20 For Holmes's entry for Friday 23 September, see *Captain Robert Holmes his Journalls of Two Voyages*, pp. 155–7. I am grateful to the Pepys Library, Magdalene College Cambridge, for giving me access to the volume.

longitude timekeepers was assured. The account was prominently reprinted in 1673 in the *Horologium Oscillatorium*, and then followed within the year by the announcement from Paris of the balance-spring watch. Huygens's impressive sequence of horological innovations – pendulum clock (1658), longitude pendulum timekeepers (1665) and balance-spring regulator (1674) – entitled him to precedence over others working close to him, and assured his lasting reputation as the pre-eminent figure in the field. The team of clock-makers, experimentalists and clock-enthusiasts, including Alexander Bruce, Lord Brouncker, Robert Hooke and Robert Moray, who had contributed significantly to his successes, faded from the record, their claims to some part of the credit, or even to feature in the story, overlooked and forgotten. Today, highly respected historians of science quote the Holmes story as the clinching evidence for Huygens's success with pendulum clocks to establish longitude with accuracy.[21]

By the time the *Horologium Oscillatorium* appeared, ostentatiously dedicated to the French king, Louis XIV, however, the Fellows of the Royal Society were of the opinion that Huygens was overstating his personal claims for priority. Immediately, strong protests were lodged by the most senior members of the Royal Society. The President, Lord Brouncker, the elder statesman of the Society, John Wallis and Sir Christopher Wren all wrote to Huygens, pointing out to him – with chapter and verse – of the contributions made to his unfolding horological theory and practice by English practitioners and virtuosi. They reminded Huygens that Robert Hooke's circular pendulum had been demonstrated and discussed at several meetings, that Alexander Bruce's modifications to the marine timekeepers had been crucial to their success, that Brouncker and Huygens had together debated the tautochronism of the cycloidal pendulum at length, that Wren had rectified the cycloid ahead of Huygens. All of these contributions were inadequately acknowledged in Huygens's work, or (in the case of Hooke) not at all.[22]

***

On 27 June 1673, the Secretary of the Royal Society Henry Oldenburg himself urged Huygens to be more generous in his acknowledgements:

> Allow me to say, that being entirely impartial and resolved to give everyone his due, insofar as I understand the matter, I find that

21 See for example Mahoney, 'Christian Huygens'.
22 See L. D. Patterson, 'Pendulums of Wren and Hooke', *Osiris* 10 (1952), 277–321; 302–5.

our Philosophers here are not inclined to claim discoveries made by others. But neither will they or anyone else take from them their inventions, or suppress what is truly theirs. . . .

You would wish me, I am sure Sir, to speak thus candidly, and so that you understand the mood of our mutual friends, who never miss an opportunity to speak well of your talents. . . . If candour reigned everywhere, what friendships might we be able to establish amongst the learned, and what advantages might the public derive?[23]

'Friendships amongst the learned', I suggest, captures the kind of Royal Society-based international collaboration which underpinned Anglo-Dutch and Anglo-French cutting-edge research on longitude timekeepers in the 1660s. Given such a strong sense of a collaborative environment, it is no wonder that Hooke and his colleagues believed that their research and development had made a significant contribution to Huygens's horological innovations, and felt cheated when he announced his 'eureka' moment, and the perfection of the balance-spring watch in 1675.

Since the discovery of the so-called 'Hooke Folio' in January 2006, we can add some further documentary evidence (more substantial than Holmes's at least) to this story.[24]

In the transcriptions Robert Hooke makes from the Journal Books and Oldenburg's rough papers in the recently rediscovered Hooke Folio Hooke particularly highlights moments when he demonstrated

23 Huygens, *Oeuvres Complètes* 7, 323–4. Bruce's response to receiving his own complimentary copy of Huygens's *Horologium Oscillatorium* was similarly critical. In the new work, Huygens described the early trials of the short-pendulum clocks, and refers to assistance from 'a certain Scottish gentleman'. Bruce was deeply wounded at this diminishing of the part he had played in the venture, and his indignation at Huygens's lack of generosity coloured the response to the new work in England, insofar as it had a bearing on longitude-timekeepers, which was largely negative, or at best indifferent. See J. H. Leopold, 'Clockmaking in Britain and the Netherlands', *Notes and Records of the Royal Society of London* 43 (1989), p. 41. Hooke also protested that Huygens had stolen the idea of an isochronous conical (or circular) pendulum from him. In the newly discovered Hooke Folio, Hooke has removed from Oldenburg's rough minutes of the Royal Society part of the entry for 28 February 1666/7, apparently as evidence that he had a good case: 'The circular pendulum designed for an equal motion with unequal weights being again spoken of, the president affirmed, that though the inventor Mr. Hooke had demonstrated, that the bullet of the circular pendulum, if it can be always kept rising or falling in a parabola, will kept its circular motion in the same time; yet he had not demonstrated, that the diameter of the parabola from the point of contact in the curve to the vertex of the diameter is equal to that portion of the curve from the said point of contact to the vertex of the same curve, *plus* half the *latus rectum* or *plus* double the focus of the parabola.'
24 http://www.livesandletters.ac.uk/cell/Hooke/Hooke.html.

key technical points at Society meetings in the presence of Huygens; he notes Oldenburg's omissions from the minutes, his failures to record key technical points made. Most dramatically, Hooke has removed two items from Oldenburg's autograph rough minutes for critical Society meetings, and added them as evidence to his own body of transcriptions. One of these concerns Hooke's demonstration of the isochronous properties of a circular pendulum, the other is four pages of rough minutes recording Hooke's demonstration of a spring-regulated watch to the Society in June 1670, and the details of its mechanism.

We were already aware of transcriptions in Hooke's hand of parts of two letters from Moray to Huygens, which Hooke had copied out from the Society's letterbooks, as evidence of Moray's letting slip vital clues to the isochronous nature of springs as demonstrated by Hooke, to Huygens. Now we find Hooke assiduously assembling the history of his contributions to what I am calling the collaborative venture of early longitude clocks and spring-regulated precision timekeepers. Taken all together, however, the volume of notes Hooke has assembled does not add up to evidence of a conscious betrayal, and I think that in the end Hooke knew this. As he puts together his dossier of occasions on which information passed from the Royal Society to Huygens (either in person, or via Moray or Oldenburg), nothing new actually emerges, either to prove once and for all that Hooke had been 'betrayed', or to clinch Hooke's own independent priority in spring-regulated timekeepers.

Indeed, I would like to think that in the course of assembling the Hooke Folio in the late 1670s, painstakingly sifting back through the documentation of ten action-packed years of scientific activity at the Royal Society, Hooke finally saw clearly the extended, collaborative Anglo-Dutch character of the whole longitude timekeeper affair, and understood the injustice of priority and acclaim being accorded to Huygens, above all the other international co-participants.

Hooke, unlike many others, down to the present day, was certainly clear that the excitement surrounding those supposedly sensational trials of Huygens's longitude pendulum clocks in 1664–5 was ill-founded, and that Holmes had tampered with the evidence. So since it is Hooke (even more than Alexander Bruce) who tends to get overlooked in the telling of the story of clocks and the quest for longitude, let me give him the last word here.

In an unpublished lecture of around 1676 (now in the British Library), Hooke, recapitulating the trials of the Bruce–Huygens clocks in which he had himself participated in early 1664, wrote:

In february <or march> 1664 as I remember my Lord Kingkarden having gotten another [pendulum clock] made here in England did togethe[r] wth. my Ld. Brounker S^r. Ro Moray & my self make a further tryall of them wth. some of ye Kings Pleasure boa[ts] but not wth. soe good successe as was expected. . . . They were afterwards sent by S^r. Robert Holmes to Guinny and an account returnd thereof somew^t. like that printed by Hugeinus <made by one of the Captaines> giving indeed a very favourable account of their performan[ce] but concealing all their faileurs & miscarriages whereas another person that was in the same ship gaue a relation very differing. which relation was concealed & the other printed.[25]

25 British Library MS Sloane 1039, fols 129–30.

4

The Reputation of Sir Constantijn Huygens: Networker or Virtuoso?

Constantijn Huygens was born in The Hague on 4 September 1596, and died there on 29 March 1687. In the Netherlands he is an iconic cultural figure for the seventeenth century – a distinguished man of letters and polymath who left an indelible mark upon emerging Dutch culture. His reputation does not, however, extend far beyond his homeland. To most readers from outside the Netherlands Huygens's name will hardly register.

In her pioneering work in the English language on Huygens, published in 1956, the literary critic Rosalie Colie wrote:

> Constantijn Huygens is almost unknown to English readers and students – if he is known at all, it is in that peculiarly frustrating and gratifying fashion, as the father of a famous son, Christiaan Huygens, the physicist. During his own lifetime, however, few Hollanders were better known outside their country than Constantijn Huygens. He has been a victim of his country's decline in international importance, and it is our loss not to know Huygens, for he was one of those many-faceted personalities who flash back to us the brilliance of their age.[1]

---

1 Rosalie L. Colie, *'Some Thankfulnesse to Constantine'. A Study of English Influence upon the Early Works of Constantijn Huygens* (The Hague: Martinus Nijhoff, 1956), p. 1. I would like to honour Colie's work here, and to recognise our shared sense of getting to know Constantijn Huygens through his prolific correspondence: 'I soon forgot to tremble when I worked among the original manuscripts of his poems or in the thick bound volumes of his letters. . . . I learned the handwritings of the Huygens family as if they were my own – the firm, clear script of Constantijn, the sharp scholar's hand of Christiaan, the loose young hand of Lodewijck. The documentation they left behind them recreated their lives; there was no escaping the Huygens family' (ibid., p. viii).

Fifty years have not changed that position a great deal. In the Netherlands, Huygens's reputation remains high, as a musician, as a poet, and as a connoisseur of the arts, not to mention his political and diplomatic career as counsellor to three generations of princes from the House of Orange.[2] Outside the Netherlands, in spite of the considerable influence I and others have argued that he wielded by virtue of his artistic and musical discernment and his prominence in political office, his name rings no bells – English-speakers cannot even agree on how to pronounce his name, though in the seventeenth century he was certainly known as 'Mr Huggins'.

Rosalie Colie called Huygens a 'Dutch virtuoso', who 'capably held his own' amongst contemporary specialists in all areas of arts and science. But she admitted that he was 'almost too good an exemplar of his time: his interests were too wide to comprehend, his manifold function too difficult to grasp'.[3] In this lecture I want to address the question as to why it seems so hard to attribute a serious and lasting international reputation to Constantijn Huygens. To anticipate my answer – because it is always easier to follow a story if the reader has some idea of where the story is leading – I shall argue that Huygens has suffered from historians' predisposition to find something heroic about the solitary genius, something rather too domestic and everyday about the networker.

Huygens, I shall show, was a consummate networker. He was also, I shall argue, a man whose activities permanently altered Europe-wide intellectual, artistic and musical tastes.[4]

***

On 8 July 1638, one of Sir Constantijn Huygens's well-connected cousins, Maarten Snouckaert van Schauburg, wrote from London with

---

2 Huygens was secretary to Frederik Hendrik and Willem II, Raad en Lid van de Nassause Domeinraad etc. See: S. Groenveld, '*Een out ende gertouw dienaer, beyde van den staet ende welstant in thuys van Orangen. Constantijn Huygens (1596–1687), een hoog Haags ambtenaar*', *Holland, regionaal-historisch tijdschrift* 20 (1988), 3–32.

3 Colie, '*Some Thankfulnesse*', p. vii.

4 In relation to Huygens's reputation, there is a particular issue associated with his acknowledgement in the period as an accomplished composer as well as performer. We know that, just as he assembled his letters and text publications for posterity, he also organised 769 compositions for various solo instruments into a volume. This, however, is now lost, and only fragments of composition survive. See L. P. Grijp, '"Te voila donc, bel oeil" An autograph tablature by Constantijn Huygens', *Tijdschrift van de Vereniging voor Nederlandse Muziekgeschiedenis* (1987), 170–4; 170; Tim Crawford, 'A composition for viola da gamba by Constantijn Huygens' and Louis Peter Grijp, 'Melodieën bij teksten van Huygens' in A.Th. van Deursen a.o. (ed.), *Veelzijdigheid als levensvorm. Facetten van Constantijn Huygens' leven en werk*, Deventer studien Volume 2 (Sub Rosa, 1987), pp. 75–88 and pp. 89–108.

the news that he was pursuing a difficult shopping errand Constantijn had set him to do while he was there. Huygens wanted to buy a consort of viols of outstanding quality for his personal use, and Snouckaert's first move had been to consult the foremost musician at the court of the English king Charles I, Nicholas Lanier.[5] His enquiry achieved gratifyingly swift results. On 24 August, Maarten was able to tell Constantijn that Lanier had indeed succeeded in locating for him 'a consort [accord] of six old viols, but the most excellent one could possible find'.

The vendor's asking price was, Maarten considered, unacceptably high. 'They are asking an outlandish price, in my opinion, that is to say, 30 pounds sterling. So I need to know as soon as possible what to do, and your last word as to what should be my highest offer. Please reply promptly to my father-in-law's house in London.'[6]

Four months later, Maarten wrote again to let Huygens know that the outcome of his extended negotiations concerning the musical instruments had been successful. First of all, the price had been confirmed as one appropriate to the quality of the purchase. Lady Stafford, to whom he had delivered a letter from Constantijn concerning the asking price, had eventually been satisfied, after examining them, that the six viols were 'extremely excellent and rare, and well worth the price asked'.

However, she had not managed to get the vendor to discount the price – probably, Maarten thought, because her careful inspection and that of her advisors had alerted the vendor to the seriousness of their interest in the goods. He, Maarten, however, as the person who was to pay for them, had driven an extremely hard bargain, and succeeded in getting the price down to 27-and-a-half pounds sterling, plus 'a grey

---

5 'Quant aux instruments d'eslite dont il vous a pleu m'escrire, je me suis adressé à un des premiers de la musique de Leurs Majestez, qui, estant fort homme de bien, m'a promis de s'en enquestrer soigneusement, espérant de trouver quelque part vostre faict.' M. Snouckaert van Schauburg to Huygens, 8 July 1638 (J. A. Worp, *De Briefwisseling van Constantijn Huygens (1608–1687)* ['s-Gravenhage 1911–1917], nr. 1881, University Library Leiden, Cod. Hug. 37, transcribed by Rasch in *Driehonderd brieven over muziek van, aan en rond Constantijn Huygens.* Bijeengebracht, ingeleid en vertaald door Rudolf Rasch [Hilversum: Verloren, 2007], 2 vols, pp. 294–5).

6 'Je vous ay escrit devant mon départ d'Angleterre . . . qu'un des premiers de la musique de Leurs Majestez, à qui je m'estoit adressé à ceste fin, avoit prins en charge et recommandation singulière la rec[h]erche des instruments d'eslite que désiriez avoir, lequel a recontré depuis, à ce qu'on m'en escrit, un accord de six violes vieilles, mais des plus excellentes que l'on puisse trouver, dont il taschera d'empescher ou retarder la vente, qu'on en veut faire, jusques à mon retour par delà. . . . Mais d'autant qu'on en demande un prix extraordinaire, à mon opinion, à sçavoir trente livres *sterling*, il sera nécessaire que je sçache le plus tost que faire se pourra combien vous voulez que j'offre au dernier mot. Partant, je vous supplie d'adresser vostre response promptement à Londres chez mon beau-père' (University Library Leiden, Cod. Hug. 37, Worp, nr. 1929, transcribed by Rasch, p. 297).

Holland [beaver] hat'. Would Huygens please send the hat as soon as the viols reached him, and he had judged them to be to his satisfaction?[7]

The six fragile musical instruments had, Snouckaert wrote, already been dispatched to Huygens, in a custom-made packing-case, and were en route to The Hague, under the watchful eye of a ship's captain from Middelburg. The total shipping price was 8 shillings, which included a trusted carrier to deliver the precious cargo safely to Huygens's door. Maarten would be grateful for speedy settlement of his bills, as he was unlikely to return to the Netherlands himself in the near future, and would have to negotiate transfer of the funds by bill of exchange.[8]

Here is an elegantly documented example of Constantijn Huygens's day-to-day involvement in what we might call 'material cultural trans-actions' between London and The Hague. His network of international connections allows him to seek out excellent examples of the most sought-after and fashionable musical instruments – instruments of recognised quality and workmanship – and to transfer them from one national context to another (thereby, we might argue, contributing to a web of musical influences from one milieu to another). On this occasion, it is a newly married cousin of Huygens's who executes the complicated commission to Huygens's instructions.

I have chosen this example deliberately because it introduces us to the part played by the expert judgement of one of Huygens's oldest London friends, named here as 'Lady Stafford', in transactions of this sort. It is her assessment of the viols (together with that of another old friend-at-a-distance of Constantijn's, an artist and musician first encountered in convivial gatherings at Lady Stafford's family home in London, Nicholas Lanier) which is critical for the completion of the deal. Together they provide the necessary expert confirmation that the deal Huygens is transacting across the Narrow Sea, as the North Sea was sometimes called, is a good one. In the case of Lady Stafford, the deal, one feels, could not have been concluded successfully without her.

'Lady Stafford' is Lady Mary Killigrew – remarried to Sir Thomas Stafford, gentleman-usher to Queen Henrietta Maria, following the death of her first husband Sir Robert Killigrew in 1633. On his second stay in England many years earlier in 1622 (the viols transaction, remember, takes place in 1638), Constantijn Huygens had struck up a lasting

---

7 For an interesting discussion of Dutch beaver hats in the period, see T. Brook, *Vermeer's Hat: The Seventeenth Century and the Dawn of the Global World* (New York: Bloomsbury Press, 2008), pp. 42–4.

8 University Library Leiden, Worp, nr. 2035, Cod. Hug. 37, transcribed by Rasch, pp. 299–300; Appendix IV.

friendship with the well-connected, welcoming Killigrew family, who were close neighbours to his diplomatic lodgings in London. Theirs was a bustling artistic household, with parents and at least eight children (the eldest about seventeen), all of whom participated in well-attended musical soirées. A talented lutenist and singer himself, Constantijn acknowledged in later life that he had been deeply and lastingly influenced by the Killigrews and their intoxicating intellectual milieu. There, alongside the royalty and nobility who regularly visited to be entertained – and in addition to the musical events in which he participated – he first met the poets John Donne and Ben Jonson, and rubbed shoulders with those we would today call 'scientists' like the Lord Chancellor Sir Francis Bacon, and the inventor and illusionist Cornelius Drebbel.[9]

Although in later life Constantijn Huygens would insist that his infatuation with the Killigrews had extended to the entire family, his surviving correspondence, and his Latin poetic autobiography, make it clear that he was particularly taken with (and emotionally entangled with) Lady Mary, with her 'snow-white throat' and 'divine voice' (as he later recalled them).[10] His unofficial fiancée back at home in The Hague, Dorothea van Dorp, was quite clear that, during the fourteen-month Dutch Embassy to London, the friendship which developed between Constantijn and Lady Mary (twelve years older than him, attractive and vivacious, mother of a brood of adorable children) was not entirely innocent.

Towards the end of Constantijn's stay Dorothea's letters to him refer pointedly to the competition between herself and Lady Killigrew. When Lady Killigrew sends her the gift of a bracelet, Dorothea retorts with emotion: 'I deserve this and more for my lending her so long what I can do without so badly.' 'I shall also have my picture dispatched to her', she goes on, though this will have to wait until a portrait she is currently

9 See A. G. H. Bachrach, *Sir Constantijn Huygens and Some Trends in the Literature and Art of Seventeenth Century England and Holland* (Thesis submitted for the Degree of DPhil in the University of Oxford, 1951). I am enormously grateful to Dr Ad Leerintveld of the Koninklijke Bibliotheek for bringing this thesis to my attention.
10 Lady Killigrew was referred to as 'the young, French' Lady Killigrew (implying some lack of morals). She appears to have been pregnant for most of Huygens's time in London (her last two children were born in 1622 and 1623), so this was no more than a flirtation. On the other hand, the decorum of their relationship was surely questionable. Even late in life, Huygens would remember his hostess with particular passionate fervour: '. . . solam, / Killigraea domus, si te cito, dixero multas. / . . . Tota domus concentus erat: pulcherrima mater, / Mater (adhuc stupeo) duodenae prolis, ab illo / Gutture tam niveo, tam nil mortale sonanti / Quam coeleste Melos Citharae sociabat, et ipso / Threïcio (dicas) animatis pollice chordis!' (Constantijn Huygens, *Mijn leven verteld aan mijn kinderen in twee boeken*. Ingeleid, bezorgd, vertaald en van commentaar voorzien door Frans R. E. Blom, Amsterdam 2003, 2 vs. Sermonum inter libros. Lib. II, 150–87, Part. 1, pp. 124–6, Part 2, pp. 216–73).

sitting for by Michael van Mierevelt is finished (if only that portrait, which she suggests elsewhere is intended for Constantijn, survived).[11] In a subsequent letter, Dorothea's barbed comments to Constantijn make her feelings about the situation very clear:

> I am sending you the amber bracelet for Lady Killigrew. I am pleased that she covets something of mine. It and all that I have in the world are hers to command. She will do it the greatest honour by wearing it, and will oblige me by doing so. Tell her this comes from someone who is her servant more than anyone has ever been, all her lovers notwithstanding. . . . Please send my respects to her gracious goodness. Tell her she may indeed believe I love her, because I am prepared to let her share the same joy as myself, and am willing to renounce my own pleasure for her sake. Do tell her so. Please do not forget the little ring she promised me.[12]

Dorothea's suspicions were evidently shared by others in the privileged circle around the Killigrews. Some years later, responding to a teasing remark in a letter from the Countess Löwenstein (or Countess of Levingstone, as he calls her in English), Huygens responded:

> I will not deny that in reminding me of Lady Stafford's kindnesses towards me you have revived in me a glimmer of those old affections; but at least rest assured, Madam, and mark it well, that there was never more than a legitimate flame in play, which could not have made anyone blush.[13]

***

Now, in case you are beginning to think that I am embroiling you in some kind of seventeenth-century Anglo-Dutch soap-opera, the point here is that Huygens's intense friendship with Lady Killigrew provided him with a trusted person to whom he could turn whenever he needed expert advice on artistic or musical commissions in London. Many years after their first flirtation, Lady Killigrew was, as we shall see, instrumental in

11 Bachrach, *Sir Constantijn Huygens,* p. 223.
12 Worp, nr. 242; Appendix IV.
13 Huygens to Lewensteyn, 23 June 1639 (Den Haag, Kon. Bibl., Hs. KA XLIX, f. 909, Worp, nr. 2136, transcribed by Bachrach, p. 352): 'Je ne dissimule pas qu'en me rememorant les bienueiullances de Mad[am]e Stafford, vous ne m'ayez vacciné quelque etincelle de ces anciennes amitiez; mais au moins, Madame, sçaurez vous, et l'aurez bien apprins pardelà, comme il n'y a eu que du feu legitime sur le jeu, et dont personne n'a que faire de rougir.'

Huygens's effecting some international exchanges of ideas and material cultural transactions which remain of considerable interest to historians today. As I try to tease out the importance of Huygens's networking on the larger intellectual and cultural historical map, these are the sorts of transactions we need to be looking at closely as we develop a model for cultural exchange and influence, facilitated by Sir Constantijn Huygens.

One of Constantijn's special talents throughout his long life, it turned out, was to survive the emotional upheavals of his intense friendships (especially with women), with the lines of personal communication between himself and his friends intact, so that he could call upon them for favours for the rest of their lives. In the present case, this is particularly true of Lady Killigrew – in spite of dramatic fallings-out with her which temporarily soured their relations, but which I have no space to deal with here. She continued her correspondence with Huygens long after he had disentangled himself from her emotionally, and formed part of Constantijn's cultural network for many decades after their initial highly charged encounter.[14]

The outcomes of these connections at a distance were frequently of some significance to cultural historians if we agree that such domestic or 'private' transactions nevertheless impact upon more public decisions taken by the participants and their circles. I suggest that the least ripple of attention paid by Huygens to artistic production elsewhere, and any inquiry he made for luxury objects and musical instruments, was of consequence, because of the prominent position he occupied at the highest levels of taste and connoisseurship at the court of the Dutch Stadholder. We can watch that influence – exerted on behalf of the leading court figures Huygens directly served – permeating the court itself, in the detail of the art commissions negotiated and purchased by Huygens on behalf of his Stadholder employers from the 1620s onwards.

Almost as soon as Frederik Hendrik assumed the Stadholdership of the United Provinces in 1625, following the death of his half-brother Maurits, he and his new wife Amalia van Solms (former lady-in-waiting to Elizabeth of Bohemia, the Winter Queen) embarked on a programme of ostentatious expenditure on luxury objects and works of art, so as to create a cultural and artistic context which would put the House of Orange in the United Provinces on the European 'royal' map. Amalia, in particular, took a close interest in the process of building up the couple's

---

14 Huygens's contact with Lady Killigrew seems to have stopped during the ten years of his marriage, but was revived (by the gift of a pair of perfumed gloves to him) shortly after his wife Susanna's death, and thereafter continued as an active relationship until her death in 1656.

collection of works of art, to establish herself and her family as 'major players' on the international courtly scene. Like collectors throughout the ages, she may have paid exorbitant sums for individual items, and accumulated art objects at a phenomenal speed, but she was nevertheless passionate about what she bought, and took lasting pleasure in paintings and decorations which it had taken time and effort for her advisors to acquire on her behalf. From the outset, the trusted artistic advisor who designed and stage-managed the court of the Stadholder and his wife was the recently appointed Secretary to Frederik Hendrik, Constantijn Huygens.[15]

Around 1626, Amalia arranged to purchase a painting by Rubens of the marriage of Roxane to Alexander the Great – a nice compliment to her new husband, who like Alexander had raised a wife from among his imperial conquests to princely rank. Huygens acted on Amalia's behalf for the acquisition. We might like to think that it was he who pointed out the appropriateness of the subject matter of the painting – a beautiful young woman plucked from obscurity to take her place beside a powerful ruler. There was once a memorandum in Rubens's handwriting among Huygens's papers, forming part of the negotiations leading to the purchase (unfortunately, it is now lost).[16]

It was an important purchase, and recognised as such at court. In 1632, we know that Rubens's 'Alexander crowning Roxane' hung in pride of place over the chimneypiece in Amalia van Solms's private cabinet (or withdrawing room) in the Stadholder's quarters in the Binnenhof at The Hague. A surviving inventory of effects in the royal palaces at the time allows us to visualise the painting in its original, intimate setting – not just a great painting by a great Flemish artist, but a treasured possession of a princess, memorialising an emotional crux in her own life. Her cabinet was entirely hung with rich green velvet, braided with gold. The same braided green velvet covered the table in the centre of the room, and the three chairs and large couch. The swagged curtains were of matching green silk. The wooden over-mantel on which the 'Alexander and Roxane' hung, was gilt on a green ground.[17] So here is Huygens

15 On the strategy of artistic magnificence used by Frederik Hendrik and Amalia to put their court on the international map, see M. Keblusek and J. Zijlmans (eds)., *Princely Display: The Court of Frederik Hendrik of Orange and Amalia Van Solms* (Zwolle: Waanders Pub., 1997); J. Israel, 'The courts of the House of Orange, c. 1580–1795', in J. Adamson (ed.), *The Princely Courts of Europe* (London: Weidenfeld and Nicolson, 1999), pp. 119–40.
16 'An autograph Memorandum from M. le Blon, in the handwriting of Rubens, Concerning a Picture for the Princess of Orange. The Subject The Marriage of Alexander the Great with Roxane'. See J. G. van Gelder, 'Rubens Marginalia IV', *The Burlington Magazine* 123 (1981), 542–6.
17 J. G. van Gelder, 'Rubens Marginalia IV', *The Burlington Magazine* 123 (1981), 542–6; 545.

helping to shape his mistress's taste (and her image), and thereby influencing that of the assiduously emulative court.

The purchase document among Huygens's papers confirmed the fact that Huygens was networking directly with Pieter Paul Rubens in the 1630s, though the two may not have met in person.

Which takes us nicely into a perhaps more unexpected area of cultural exchange in which Huygen's long-distance network of epistolary transactions turns out to have played a significant part – building design and the seventeenth-century revival of neo-classical architecture.

In view of his contacts with Rubens during negotiations for paintings for Frederik Hendrik and Amalia, and the fact that Huygens had family property near Antwerp, and made regular visits there, it is not altogether surprising that when Huygens himself set about the construction of a substantial family home in The Hague in the 1630s he should have written to Rubens in Antwerp for an expert opinion on the plans. The painter had recently added an impressive neo-classical wing to his own house on the Wapper canal. Huygens's house and the adjacent Mauritshuis, whose construction he also oversaw on behalf of its owner, were designed in the latest neo-classical style, by Jacob van Campen.[18]

On 2 July 1639, Huygens sent Rubens a set of engravings of his completed house built next door to the Mauritshuis in the most fashionable district in The Hague, Het Plein: 'Here as I promised is the bit of brick that I have built at The Hague.'[19] He is palpably proud of the landmark building he has created, and eager for the approval of Rubens as a connoisseur of antique and modern buildings. Rubens replied, giving his positive assessment in some detail, and Huygens drafted an equivalently detailed response. The exchange was cut short, however, by Rubens's death in 1640.[20]

18 'Enfin, Monsieur, je bastis à la Haye, et me seroit chose de beaucoup de contentement d'entendre voz adviz sur mes ordonnances, quoyque desjà executées, à deux petites galeries près, qui doibvent enfermer une bassecour, longue 70 pieds, et s'attacher à un front de logis, qui en a hors d'oeuvre pres de 90. Vous ne serez pas marry d'apprendre, que je pretens faire revivre là dessus un peu d'architecture anciene, que je cheris de passion, mais ce n'est qu'au petit pied, et jusqu'à où le souffrent le climat et mes coffres. Tant y a, au chaud de ces contemplations, je ne doibs guere prendre de peine à vous faire croire le desir que j'auroy de vous gouverner chez moy, qui excellez en la cognoissance de ceste illustre estude, comme en toute autre chose, et m'en pourriez faire des leçons, *sed fata obstant*. . . . Selon qu'elles reussiront, j'auray à faire ou non, scrupule de vous asseurer en paper ou de bouche, que je suis passionement . . . [13?] November 1635' (Worp, nr. 1301). See also: F. R. E. Blom, H. G. Bruin and K. A. Ottenheym, *Domus. Het huis van Constantijn Huygens in Den Haag* (Zutphen: Walburg Pers, 1999), pp. 69–70.

19 Worp, nr. 2149; Appendix IV.

20 See K. A. Ottenheym, 'De correspondentie tussen Rubens en Huygens over architectuur (1635–1640)', *Bulletin K.N.O.B.* (1997), 1–11.

This important piece of international architectural cross-fertilisation has been noted already by the architectural historian Koen Ottenheym. What has not, so far as I am aware, been noticed, is that Rubens was not the only architectural expert who was the recipient of a set of engravings of his new mansion. The correspondence with Rubens is part of a more extensive, carefully planned campaign for circulating Huygens's precious engravings of his new house beyond the United Provinces. Significantly, we find that he had arranged for them to be sent to Lady Stafford – Lady Mary Killigrew, now in her sixties – for the express purpose of her passing them to her close acquaintance, the English royal architect of the Banqueting House in Whitehall, Inigo Jones.

A week before Huygens sent the bundle of engravings of his new house to Rubens, he wrote a long letter to Lady Stafford concerning his spacious and elegant new residence. This letter contains a vivid description of the house itself, and a pressing invitation for his old friend to visit him and the court of Elizabeth of Bohemia.[21] '[The house] is nothing less then a Pallace', he writes, its elegance and symmetry worth a trip across the English Channel:

> If y^u take the paynes to consider this little building, y^u will find it of an equall proportion of both sides. The reason was that I made it for two parties. The one was my deare Bedd-fellow, and the other I, so that neither o^{ur} people nor companies that should come to visit us could hinder one another. Now that God hath depriued me of her, the left hand is left for a Cousine of mine that gouerneth my children, and the right hand towards the garden serueth to my owne use.... And certainly I dare bragge, if the shape of the Howse doe not please y^e, you will like the situation and acknowledge it standeth in a faire and sweete place, as any could be wished.[22]

In spite of Constantijn's elaborately courteous insistence that Lady Stafford must visit the house in person, the substance of this letter is

---

21 Lady Stafford's second husband was part of the household of Queen Henrietta Maria. Huygens's effusive encouragement for Lady Stafford to visit Elizabeth of Bohemia is part of his consistent activity on behalf of the Winter Queen, cementing relations between herself and her sister-in-law in England. Since part of my argument here is that Lady Killigrew was a formidable figure in her own right, we might note that in 1652 it was she who negotiated the sale of the Carew Manuscripts, which had passed into her second husband's possession, shortly before she left England to join her son Thomas Killigrew and his Dutch wife in Maastricht, where she died in 1656.

22 Huygens to Lady Stafford, 24 June 1639, Den Haag, Kon. Bibl., Hs. KA XLIX, f. 52, Worp, nr. 2138, transcribed by Bachrach, pp. 352–3.

to ask her to do him a favour in London. It alerts her to the imminent arrival of a set of engravings of the house, which he wants her to pass to the appropriate recipients – 'I cannot chose but acknowledge myself most strictly bound to y^u for so great a fauour, by these lines; wch are to serue with all for the conueyance of some figures cutt in brasse upon the modell of my howse, built by me lately at the Haghe.'

Four days later we find a letter from Huygens (this time in French) to Sir William Boswell, English Ambassador to The Hague and currently about to leave Holland for London, with instructions concerning the dispatch of the engravings:

> For the rest Sir, this large packet will let you know how seriously I take the compliment friends like yourself make me, when they offer their friendship and good offices. It contains the engravings of my paltry piece of Architecture, which I already promised to Lady Killigrew (now Stafford). I would be glad to know how I may manage to get them past Dunkirk, where I would hate it to be said that I had merely the intention of exerting myself to send them. Now that your people are transporting more than one trunk for you, I very humbly beseech you to find a corner in the least important of them for this roll of papers, and ask that a lackey may be found on your arrival to deliver them. I have added a second set of drawings for your pains, knowing well how on journeys like these one needs quantities of spare paper for wrapping up one's belongings.[23]

To complete the details of the transaction Huygens is here setting up, we have to turn to an earlier letter he sent to one of Lady Stafford's oldest and closest friends, from the period when they all knew one another in London in the 1620s, Sir John Finett.[24] There, in another elaborate conceit, in the course of passing a sequence of messages on his part to Lady Stafford, he tells Finett that he has no room on the page he is sending to give a full description of the beauties of his just-completed house in Het Plein, but that he will shortly be able to do better, when he sends a set of engravings:

> I will shortly inform you more fully, but it will be without the redundancy of words. A set of engravings will explain to

23 28 June 1639, Den Haag, Kon. Bibl., Hs. KA XLIX, f. 903, Worp, nr. 2145, transcribed by Bachrach, pp. 354–5; Appendix IV.
24 I am accepting Bachrach's identification of the recipient of this letter as Finett.

you where I am now living. Furthermore (since I am being provocative) Mr Inigo Jones will thereby learn, if he pleases, that the true Vitruvius is not altogether exiled from Holland.[25]

In a postscript, Huygens makes clear that this request for assistance is intended for Lady Stafford, and that he uses Finett as an intermediary out of decorum, in view of the fact that Huygens was in deep mourning following the death of his wife Susanna.

Architectural historians take a particularly close interest in the circulation and transmission from one location to another of plans and elevations of important new buildings. These provide concrete evidence of design influence crossing national boundaries, and shaping the buildings produced even by those who are not able (in spite of Huygens's insistence) to travel to see the products of the designs themselves. In other words, architectural 'influence' is accepted by architectural historians as travelling from place to place via drawings and engravings, even today. This epistolary evidence that engravings of Van Campen's important neo-classical home designed for Sir Constantijn Huygens circulated both to Rubens in Antwerp and (if we are to believe this correspondence) via Lady Stafford to Inigo Jones and his circle in London is certainly intriguing.

***

We are building up a picture of a web of connections and trans-actions going on between The Hague and London, facilitated by Huygens's multi-lingual correspondence, and the shuttling to and fro of trusted friends and acquaintances. Here is one more, of which I am particularly fond, which shows rather dramatically how a set of exchanges among Huygens's letters can recover fascinating glimpses of overlooked instances of high-profile material cultural exchange. This time, Huygens's trusted correspondents and carriers are the Duarte family from Antwerp, and the catalyst for the flurry of activity is the

---

25 'Dans quelque temps toutefois je vous en entretiendray: mais ce sera sans parler. une taille douce vous ira dire ou j'habite. de mesme (puisque je suis en train d'enrager) Mr Inigo Jones le sçaura s'il luy plaist pour apprendre que le vray Vitruuius n'est pas detout exilé d'Hollande'. Huygens to [Finett], 21 November 1637 (Kon. Bibl., Hs. KA XLIX, p. 748, Worp, nr. 1765, author's transcription). Huygens's postscript emphasises the fact that in spite of the decorum (in mourning as Huygens is) of addressing Finett, the communication and its instructions are for Lady Stafford: 'Le cher Snouckaert, mon tres proche parent, s'est voulu charger de l'adresse immediate de ma response à Madame Staffort. C'est ce qui vous en garantit, Monsieur, pour ceste fois, mais je doubte fort que vous ne l'eschappiez pas toujours si belle.'

impending marriage of Princess Mary Stuart, daughter of Charles I, to Prince William II of Orange, Frederik Hendrik's only son.

The Sephardic art-lover and entrepreneur Gaspar Duarte was born in Antwerp in 1584. His family had come to the city as refugees, escaping religious persecution in Lisbon. Duarte built a flourishing business in gems and artworks, and around 1632 he established a business outlet in London, where he and his sons Diego and Jacob were granted 'denizen' status as nationalised Englishmen in 1634. Between 1632 and 1639 Gaspar Duarte was jeweller (and gem procurer and supplier) to Charles I – a position which effectively made him agent for Charles's purchases and disposals of gemstones. He relocated the business to Antwerp after the outbreak of the Civil War, but remained in touch with many of his old clients from London.

In March 1641, Gaspar Duarte wrote from Antwerp to Huygens in The Hague. The letter (in French) contains an appropriate amount of musical small talk (the two men are exchanging the scores of Italian songs for one or more voices), but a substantive item of Stadholder business takes up most of it.

Duarte writes to let Huygens know that, as requested by representatives of Frederik Hendrik, his son Jacob in London has located a particularly striking and expensive piece of jewellery – an elaborate brooch in the latest fashionable style, comprising four individual diamonds in a complicated setting, and designed to be worn on the stomacher of a woman's dress.[26]

The piece is to be a sensational gift for Frederik Hendrik's teenage son William to present to his bride-to-be, Charles I's nine-year-old daughter Mary Stuart, on the occasion of their marriage in London that May. Duarte in Antwerp tells Huygens in The Hague that he has identified the perfect piece for this purpose in London:

> One of my friends, Sir Arnout Lundi, has asked me for an important jewel ['joiau'] worth 80,000 florins, on behalf of His Highness, the Prince of Orange. I had delivered to the said Sir Lundi a mock-up [plomb] and pattern of a rich jewel, a fortnight ago, to show to His Highness, by way of a gentleman, a friend of the aforementioned Lundi, called Mr. Joachim Fiqfort. So far

---

26 This is not the only occasion on which we find Huygens involved in trafficking diamonds between London and The Hague. In June 1639 he took advantage of the Countess Löwenstein's travelling between the two towns, to have two diamonds safely transported to him for the Stadholder. Huygens to Lewensteyn, 23 June 1639 (Den Haag, Kon. Bibl., Hs. KA XLIX, f. 909, Worp, nr. 2136, transcribed by Bachrach, p. 351).

I have received no response. So your cousin advised me that it would be a good thing if I let yourself know about this, so that you could alert His Highness not to buy any other piece of equivalent value until he has seen this one. It is in London in the control of my son, who, if I instruct him to do so, will himself convey it to you. Their honours the Holland ambassadors saw it in London, and also told His Highness about it, because they were so delighted to see so magnificent a piece. For the four diamonds in combination have the impact of a single diamond of value 1 million florins.[27]

On 7 April, Gaspar Duarte's son Jacob arrived in Antwerp with the jewel in his possession, and the following day Huygens examined it himself. A fortnight later, with Huygens discreetly facilitating the process, the deal had made progress. Huygens has agreed to take the jewel to The Hague:

I remain greatly indebted to you [Duarte wrote to Huygens] for the great affection you have shown towards my son Jacob Duarte, by tomorrow showing His Highness that beautiful jewel which I mentioned to you previously. And although I understand that Mr. Alonse de Lope has already managed to sell His Highness four other pieces [of expensive jewellery], nevertheless I hope that your particular favour will have the power to be successful in this matter, since this is such an extraordinarily rare piece. It would be most gracious of you to represent [to His Highness] how thus far I see small appearance [of successful completion], not having been made an offer which is reasonable, [but] one much lower than what it cost me.

However, Duarte continues, the Stadholder's suggested best offer for it is still too low to be acceptable:

Which disappoints me, not thereby being able to serve His Highness. I was assured that His Majesty [the king] of England would have been more delighted with this piece than with all the other jewels, since he had already made an offer for it himself to my younger son, by way of Milord Chamberlain, if his brother had arrived in time. For His Majesty had even offered 6,500 pounds

27   G. Duarte to Huygens, Antwerp, 24 March 1641 (Worp, nr. 2677).

sterling, and would never imagine that His Highness could have acquired it for less.[28]

Duarte's suggestion that the English king was interested in the piece was a shrewd piece of commercial pressuring, and apparently clinched the deal. On 9 May, Duarte acknowledged receipt of payment by Huygens on the Stadholder's behalf.

The exchanges of letters concerning Princess Mary's wedding gift present us with the intriguing picture of a luxury object whose value – financially and in terms of current taste – is being established by reference to its desirability in two locations, inside two fashionable societies. Given his non-royal status, the Dutch Stadholder needs a gift which will greatly impress the English king. His agent has identified a suitably extravagant jewel which is actually in London, conveniently in the possession of a Dutch diamond dealer. The piece has already been admired by the English king.

The Duartes are suppliers of gems and made-up pieces of jewellery to Charles I in London and Frederik Hendrik in The Hague. They also, again conveniently, have close family friends in place to help facilitate the deal – Joachim of Wicquefort, otherwise known as Joachim Factor, was a friend of Gaspar Duarte's daughter Francesca, and part of the Duarte 'firm'. Huygens provides his expert assessment and confirmation for the deal.

On 19 April 1641, Prince William, with an entourage of 250 people, made landfall in England at Gravesend, and proceeded to London for his wedding. Some days later he was received in Whitehall Palace, where he presented members of the royal party with diamonds, pearls and other jewellery, worth almost £23,000. These included the spectacular jewel for his bride whose purchase Huygens had helped negotiate in London, and which she wears on the front of her silver wedding dress in the famous Van Dyck portrait of the young couple. Less than a year later, at the outbreak of the English civil wars, when Princess Mary and her mother joined her young husband in The Hague, the jewel went with them. Thus in the space of a year, this distinctive, exquisitely designed and executed, expensive piece of jewellery crossed the Narrow Sea three times.

In the correspondence between Huygens and Gaspar Duarte about the iconic wedding-gift brooch, a sale of Constantijn Huygens's own becomes intertwined with his expensive dealings on behalf

28   G. Duarte to Huygens, 21 April 1641 (Worp, nr. 2694).

of the Stadholder. This gives us a clear sense of the extent of Huygens's personal involvement and influence in the cultural life of the Stadholder's court, and deserves a mention here. Duarte informs Huygens of the progress being made in selling a substantial piece of property just outside Antwerp – the Lanternhof – belonging to Huygens's family. Duarte is acting as agent in this sale also, and in the same letter in which he notifies Huygens of the discovery of the jewel, tells him that he thinks he has found a suitable buyer in his own financial deal, whom he would like to show round the property.[29] The house was indeed sold around the time Huygens agreed to the purchase of the brooch, and the speedy financial settlement of the Stadholder's purchase seems to have been achieved by using the funds from Huygens's house sale – either directly in settlement of the bill, or as security for it.[30]

Huygens's correspondence shows that the scattered Duarte family also acted, in similar series of exchanges, as expert negotiators for the purchase of a harpsichord for Huygens, and one might want to argue that Huygens's correspondence network is built most robustly on the provision of advice and assistance for musical transactions, from which others naturally follow.[31] The outcome, in any case, is the same. Supported by his dispersed, trusted, expert advisors, Constantijn Huygens intervenes directly in a key purchase associated with the Stuart–Orange marriage of 1641 to assure the high-profile stylishness of an iconic gift from a Dutch aspiring prince to an English princess. Once again, we might note, that transaction involves participants traditionally undervalued or overlooked in historians' discussions of the formation of taste – this time a family of emigré Sephardic Jews.

***

Not all Constantijn Huygens's cultural and artistic interventions were, however, as successful as those I have so far chosen to pick out from his voluminous correspondence. I will complete this series of (what I hope are) telling examples of his cross-cultural influence, therefore, with an

---

29 G. Duarte to Huygens, Antwerp, 24 March 1641 (Worp, nr. 2677).
30 There is more research to be carried out on the financial transactions surrounding the brooch and Lanternhof sales. In two letters in August 1644, one of Huygens's brothers-in-law is still referring to the papers concerning the sale of the Lanternhof, and the transfer of money from that sale between Antwerp and The Hague. Worp incorrectly believes that this is the date at which the house was sold. It is more likely that bills of exchange associated with that sale are still being used in Huygens's financial business as conducted between The Hague and Antwerp. See Worp, nrs 3683 and 3730.
31 See Rasch, *Driehonderd brieven*.

account of an attempted cultural exchange of some ostentation initiated by Huygens which he failed to complete to his own satisfaction.

In early April 1645, the royal lutenist at the English court wrote in response to an inquiry from Huygens:

> You have done me the honour of asking me to find you a Bologna lute with nine ribs. I must tell you, sir, that all the Bologna lutes with nine ribs are by Laux Maler, who died 120 years ago, and are mostly of medium size and not suitable to accompany a singer. And I do not believe that there are more than fifty surviving in the entire world. As for here [in London] I am sure there are not more than six.[32]

Jacques Gaultier had been formally introduced to Huygens in August 1630 (the letter of introduction from Jacob van der Burgh is in the Huygens archive in Leiden), though they had probably already met at the Killigrew home in 1622.[33] Fifteen years later, he has become a member of the extended network of expert-at-a-distance acquaintances who can assist Huygens in his latest musical shopping quest. This time it is a search for a Laux Maler lute of great rarity and exceptional musical quality, which Huygens wants to acquire for his own use.

Shortly after this first letter about the lute quest, Gaultier wrote again. He had, after all, managed to track down a Laux Maler, nine-ribbed lute:

> It turns out that this lute is absolutely the most handsome and the best Bologna lute that there is in England, of the size you are after, on the larger side, rather than small. It has nine ribs and is by Laux Maler. It is fretted and provided with a pegbox [enmanché] by Master Nichols, who is recognised here as the finest there is at fretting. And for the rest too, it is a lute suitable for singing to, as well as for playing instrumental pieces.[34]

---

32 'Vous m'avez faict l'honneur de me commander de vous trouver un luth de Boulogne à neuf côttes. Je vous diray, Monsieur, que tous les luths de Boulogne à 9 côttes sont de Laux Maller, qui est mort il y a [cent]-vingt ans, et sont tous la pluspart de moiyenne taille et non propre pour chanter. Et croy qu'il n'y en a en tout le monde cinquante. Pour icy je suis certain qu'il n'y en a pas six'. Jacques Gaultier to Huygens, 20 March 1645. University Library Leiden, Cod. Hug 37, Worp, nr. 3928, transcribed by Rasch, pp. 717–18.

33 Worp, nr. 523, transcribed by Rasch, p. 265. See also Rasch p. 170 for Gaultier's career.

34 Gaultier to Huygens, c. 30 April 1645. University Library Leiden, Cod. Hug 37, Worp, nr. 3953, transcribed and replaced in the right 'Worp' order as nr. 3940A by Rasch, pp. 719–20; Appendix IV.

The owner of this outstanding instrument was prepared to part with it for thirty pounds sterling, Gaultier told Huygens. He was also willing to have the lute sent to The Hague, where Huygens could try it out at his leisure. Should he not be satisfied with it, it could be returned, providing it was in perfect condition when it arrived back in London.

The lute was eventually dispatched to Huygens, who decided not to purchase it. Gaultier's next letter reported that it had been safely returned, and the vendor was happy to return the asking price. We hear no more of Laux Maler lutes for four years. But in 1649, in the aftermath of the English civil wars, and within months of the execution of King Charles I, Gaultier contacted Huygens again. This time he offered Huygens King Charles I's own Laux Maler, nine-ribbed lute. Once again, he had sought Lady Stafford's advice before contacting Huygens:

> So, Sire, concerning the lute you wanted me to find for you. Lady Stafford discussed it with me, without arriving at a decision, feeling uneasy about it. If you want my reasoning: the said lute has been chosen from among a quantity of others coming from Bologna, and is the only one by Laux Maler who died 150 years ago. It was bought by a man named John Ballard, lutenist to His Majesty, and cost him 60 pistols for the body and [table] alone. Since then he has had it repaired and brought it to England. During Ballard's lifetime the king could not gain possession of the lute by any means. When Ballard died, and the lute remained with his poor family, they decided after much discussion to sell it to the king for 100 pounds sterling.
>
> And afterwards the king gave it to me as the only recompense for 30 years of service. . . . I would not let it go at any price for anyone but yourself. . . . And if you decide you want it, the price will be what it cost the king.[35]

Once again, this royal lute was dispatched to The Hague 'on approval', for Huygens's personal inspection. On this occasion, Constantijn had

35   Gaultier to Huygens, early 1649. University Library Leiden, Cod. Hug. 37, Worp, nr. 5223, transcribed and renumbered as Worp, nr. 4950A by Rasch, pp. 944–5; Appendix IV. See also Gautier to Huygens, August 1649, London, Brit. Libr., Ms. Add. 15944, fols 46–7, Worp, nr. 3708 [= 4970A] as transcribed by Rasch, p. 947: 'Vous me dites par la vostre, Monseigneur, que le désirez comparer. . . . Je vous prie, Monseigneur, de ne trouver rude que je traite avec vous de pris, pourquoy, que se soit qui soit à moy, je vous priray de ragarder l'estat de ma fortune après trent années de service à un si grand roy et royne que je n'ay rien à montrer que ce luth.'

indicated that he wanted to compare its tone with that of another which had been found for him in Paris (as a result of Huygens's usual practice of sending out inquiries to more than one expert correspondent). This time the nine-rib Laux Maler lute had been located, examined and appraised by the French royal organist Pierre de la Barre, father of the virtuoso musician Anne de la Barre. De la Barre had in fact already asked for a second opinion from his compatriot Gaultier before bringing it to Huygens' attention.[36]

Huygens did not buy Gaultier's over-priced London lute, in spite of the glowing recommendations with which it came to him. Nor, it seems, did he ever find the Laux Maler, nine-ribbed instrument of his dreams (in the late 1670s he was still inquiring after one, this time in Spain, where the fashion for guitars had depressed the price of lutes).

I like to think that, in spite of its exquisite sound and quality, Huygens returned the English royal lute to the now-unemployed and hard-up Jacques Gaultier because he felt uneasy at the way it had come to him – part of the process of settling outstanding payments to individuals (as salaries or debts) at the time of the king's imprisonment and subsequent execution.[37] Gaultier had, after all, reported that on this occasion Lady Mary Killigrew's approval of the purchase had not been forthcoming: 'Lady Stafford discussed it with me, without arriving at a decision, feeling uneasy about it [estant malaise].' Staunch supporter of the Stuart dynasty, Huygens would, I feel sure, have shared her queasiness at the manner in which this lute – however outstanding its musical quality – had come into Gaultier's possession. How could Huygens ever have performed in front of the Princess Royal, Mary Stuart (Charles I's daughter) or Elizabeth of Bohemia (Charles I's sister) on an instrument acquired under such macabre circumstances?

***

So what can we conclude from this excursion through the letters of Constantijn Huygens, and the network of deals and acquisitions he

---

36 'Suivant donc ce que vous m'avez mandé, j'ay fait perquisition chez tous ceux qui ont des luths de Bologne à vendre. J'en ay trouvé deux de la mesme taille de la mesure que vous m'avez envoyez, dont l'un est de Laux Maler à neuf costes. Il est excellent d'harmonie, mais, comme il est fort vieil, il est bien cassé et mesme il y a quelques pieces. Son prix est de quinze pistolles pour le plus. . . . Mais en cette affaire, de peur de se mesprendre, suivant la resolution que vous manderez, jer prieray Monsieur Gautier et d'autres excellents Messieurs de me dire leurs advis, car j'ay toujours ouy dire qu'il vaut mieux faillir avec conseil que de bien faire de soy-mesme' (Den Haag, Kon. Bibl., Hs. KA XLIIaa, nr. 96, Worp, nr. 4886, transcribed by Rasch, p. 917).

37 See J. Brotton, *The Sale of the Late King's Goods: Charles I and His Art Collection* (London: Macmillan, 2006).

brokered or presided over with the assistance of his scattered, trusted, intimate correspondents? I hope the small sample of stories of such cultural exchanges and transactions that I have recovered from the archives may have persuaded you of the richness, depth and texture of the web of these relationships. In my view, as multiplied again and again across Huygens's prolific correspondence, over sixty or so years, this constitutes a contribution of real, considerable importance towards the emergence of a characteristically Anglo-Dutch culture during the same period.

Because of the collaborative nature of each and every one of the cultural events I have documented here, there is a reluctance on the part of historians to identify Sir Constantijn Huygens as fully instrumental in their formation, rather than as some kind of catalyst for a 'shared' (and thus, by implication, less significant) contribution to the history of culture. I believe I have argued here for an alternative view – that each and every one of these exchanges emanated from Huygens himself, was master-minded and controlled by him, and produced an outcome of which he can be considered to have had full historical ownership.

As I suggested at the beginning of this exploration of Huygens's reputation, his network of close friendships with experts in every field of culture placed him in a central position in the cultural activities of his day, but the diversity of his interests has subsequently prevented the scale of his influence from being recognised. Political historians have noted Huygens as a civil servant, art historians have claimed a part for him in the 'discovery' of Rembrandt, historians of the Reformation have argued for his influence in shaping Dutch faith, linguists have praised his poetic language, Renaissance scholars his contribution to a Dutch Renaissance. The web of connections which I have described here weaves and interweaves these areas into a formidably dense, richly colourful tapestry. I want to argue strongly that this is Huygens's true and lasting contribution to history.

Huygens may have been, first and foremost, a consummate networker, using a Europe-wide set of connections assiduously to bind contacts and friends to his varied and wide-ranging interests. But the enduring impact and ramifications of his web of influence raises him, surely, as Rosalie Colie maintained, to the lasting stature and importance of Holland's foremost and most widely remembered virtuoso.

5

'Dear Song': Scholarly Whitewashing of the Correspondence between Constantijn Huygens and Dorothea van Dorp

I want here to explore the self-fashioning of a successful seventeenth-century individual via the written form most typical of self-awareness in the period – the familiar letter. Nowhere is that image-shaping more energetic, pragmatic and, we might say, obvious than in Constantijn Huygens's early personal life, as this ambitious young member of the élite circle in The Hague explored every available avenue of patronage and service, so as to assure himself a successful and privileged future career.[1] Yet precisely here, it seems, scholars have tended to turn a blind eye to the amount of self-construction involved in crafting his meteoric rise. Rather than subjecting the early letters to close critical scrutiny, they have preferred to accept Constantijn's self-evaluation – as a virtuous, unassuming, amiable sort of a fellow – at face value. They have, furthermore, largely used Huygens's highly contrived early poems as the biographical basis for their account.[2]

1 Huygens's early letters home to his parents from his embassy trips abroad are full of descriptions of his manoeuvring to secure himself a desirable official appointment, and he displays considerable self-consciousness about this: 'Il faut que le contentement cede un peu à la necessité, mon tour viendra s'il plait à Dieu' (J. A. Worp, *De Briefwisseling van Constantijn Huygens (1608–1687).* ['s-Gravenhage 1911–1917] nr. 25 [not transcribed]). In a letter to his parents (usually his enthusiastic supporters in every move to secure a future role for himself at court) written in January 1622, Huygens responds to a rebuke from them which suggests that even they are finding his aspirations towards preferment excessive. They have, it seems, commented on his high-blown language: 'Je ne considere point sur quoy se fonde la reproche de mon stile affetté. Certes, quand l'envie m'en prendroit, le loisir m'en reculeroit bien. C'est une vanité que j'ay tousjours detestée en autruy, evitée en moy mesme. Aussi n'est ce point devers mes parents que je presumeroye d'en user. Je pense m'estre esvertué au possible, en vous faisant entendre ce qui me vient au devant en aussi peu de paroles que les affaires de mes maistres me permettent de jetter à la haste; d'affiquets ou de fard ne croyez pas que je m'y mette. Ce seroit me friser les cheveux, où à grand peine ay-je loisir à me les peigner' (Worp, nr. 120).
2 On Huygens's life, see most recently J. Smit, *De grootmeester van woord- en snarenspel. Het leven van Constantijn Huygens* (The Hague: Martinus Nijhoff, 1980). On Huygens and

In many ways, this is surprising. There are plenty of clues to be found in Constantijn's early poems revealing the extent of his self-conscious efforts towards appropriate presentation of himself and his emotions for success in public life at this time. Thus, for example, Jan Bloemendal and Ad Leerintveld have elegantly excavated the way he uses contemporary, typically Dutch emblem books, such as Otto Vaenius's *Amorum Emblemata*, to construct a highly wrought, conventionally recognisable version of the emotional bond between himself and the 'girl next door', Dorothea van Dorp, as a virtuous friendship, in his January 1619 poem 'Is 't quelling sonder maet'.[3] Each stanza of that poem – which he may have presented in manuscript as a gift to Dorothea – is contrived from a carefully chosen emblem, so as to craft and locate their feelings for one another into a form identifiable within a well-understood contemporary context, thereby proposing a passionate commitment directed towards spiritual and intellectual, rather than worldly (let alone carnal) goals.

Bloemendal and Leerintveld prefer not to reach a conclusion as to the motive behind Huygens's flamboyantly erudite verses. I suggest that 'Is 't quelling sonder maet' is a well-executed example, carefully matched to contemporary expectations (the very basis for a plausible self-fashioning) for the consumption of those around the pair who might remark on their intimacy, of the poetic re-presentation of an actual love affair as a conventional, appropriately chaste, morally admirable and decorous, socially acceptable literary relationship.

Although not a reliable source of the 'facts' behind the Huygens Dorp affair, Huygens's poetry may give us some pointers towards decoding their contemporary epistolary exchanges. The careful

Dorothea van Dorp, see J. A. Alberdingk Thijm, 'Constantin Huygens en de familie van Dorp', *De Dietsche Warande* (1864) 465–89, and 'Constantin Huygens. Onuitgegeven Hss. en nadere letterkundige bizonderheden. Nog iets over Dorothea van Dorp', *De Dietsche Warande* (1869) 477–82; J. A. Worp, 'Brieven van Constantijn Huygens aan Dorothea van Dorp', *De Dietsche Warande* (1892) 335–44; F. L. Zwaan, 'Huygens en Dorothea', *Tijdschrift voor Nederlandse Taal- en Letterkunde* 98 (1982) 131–6; E. Keesing, *Het volk met lange rokken. Vrouwen rondom Constantijn Huygens* (Amsterdam: Querido, 1987) and 'Hoe is het met Dorothée van Dorp verder gegaan?', *De Zeventiende Eeuw* 3 (1987), 115–24. On Dorothea van Dorp, see J. M. L. Lechanteur: 'Dorp, Dorothea van', in *Digitaal Vrouwenlexicon van Nederland*, http://www.inghist.nl/Onderzoek/Projecten/DVN/lemmata/data/DorotheavanDorp.

3 J. Bloemendal and A. Leerintveld, 'De "Literaire" vriendschap tussen Constantijn Huygens en Dorothea van Dorp: Een verliefde jongen te rade bij een emblematicus?', *Spiegel der Letteren* 47 (2005), 275–85. See also A. Leerintveld (ed.), *Constantijn Huygens, Nederlandse gedichten 1614–1625. Historisch-kritische uitgave, verzorgd door Ad Leerintveld*, 2 vols (Den Haag: Constantijn Huygens Instituut, 2001), Monumenta Literaria Neerlandica 12, 1–2. For a full, commented version of Vaenius's *Amorum Emblemata* (1608), see the full text and transcription in the collection of online emblem books at Utrecht University: http://emblems.let.uu.nl/v1608.html.

composition of the poem I refer to indicates, perhaps, that by 1619 Constantijn had made up his mind that marriage to Dorothea (whom he had first met in 1614) was not advisable, or even a real possibility, if he was to achieve his career ambitions.[4] In April 1618, almost a year before he composed his emblematic celebration of his love for Dorothea, Huygens had already acknowledged what he considered to be the limitations of this close attachment in writing. In a letter to his mother, he had reassured her that he was not about to rush into marriage. Rather, he would take parental advice and wait until he had found a suitably well-placed, wealthy bride before committing himself:

> The marriage of Van de Weerde, so one hears, is a certainty. His bride is a rich heiress, whom he is going to marry in spite of all those rejected suitors [blauwscheenen heers] who did not expect it to turn out that way. As for myself, I kiss your hands for the good advice you have given me, to look for a bride for myself at an equivalent price. When the prospect is 100,000 francs, I have no inclination to hang myself so early.[5]

As if to consolidate this determination, three months later, while comfortably settled in the residence of Noel de Caron, heer van Schoonewal, in London during his first embassy attachment there, Huygens wrote a pastoral poem, 'Doris oft Herder-clachte' (Doris, or the shepherd's complaint), which again effects the distancing of himself emotionally from any sort of on-going 'real', publicly recognised 'betrothal' or commitment. In this poem, the shepherd weeps for the loss of his beloved Doris, for whom he professes undying love, but a love which will be unrequited, because the object of his love, who had promised herself to him, has spurned his affections and rejected him for another man. By this means he (the authorial voice) can play or perform histrionically as a lover, without there being any danger (supposedly) that his intentions will be misunderstood.

---

4 Shortly after his family moved into a new home on the Voorhout in 1614, Huygens wrote in his commonplace book (Dagboek): 'Dorothea innotui'. He notes his first meeting with Anna Roemers Visscher in the same words in 1619.

5 'Le mariage de Van de Weerde à ce qu'on tient est asseuré; c'est une riche heritiere qu'il va espouser au despit de beaucoup de Blauwscheen-Heers qui n'avoyent point attendu leur cassade de ce coté la. Pour ce qui est de moy, je vous baise les mains pour le bon advis que me donnez, d'en chercher une pour moy au mesme prix. Quand la potence vaudroit 100000 francs, je n'ay pas envie de me faire pendre de si bonne heure' (Worp, nr. 43). 'De Zierixzee, cet 11e d'Avr. 1618.' Another letter to his parents, a few months later, testifies to the intimacy that at this time certainly exists between Constantijn and Dorothea. Worp, nr. 56, in Rasch, 257–8; Appendix V 'De South-Lambeth, ce 7e de Septembre 1618, Viel Stile'.

Critics have identified this poem also as autobiographical, and used it to maintain that the lovesick Huygens was actually jilted by Dorothea while he was away in England, but there is, to my knowledge, no extra-literary evidence that this was really the case. Indeed, as we shall see, a full nine years later the official announcement that Huygens himself was to be married to somebody else – the much more socially suitable, and wealthier, Susanna van Baerle – which apparently reached Dorothea only weeks before their engagement, came as a complete shock to his 'friend' and caused outrage to Dorothea's family. It may have caused lasting strain between the two households, located close to one another on the Voorhout in The Hague.[6]

By 1619, then, whatever his conduct towards Dorothea in private, or, indeed, her personal understanding and expectations, Constantijn Huygens had already honed to his satisfaction the 'official' version of his relationship with Dorothea van Dorp, fashioning it into a recognisable seventeenth-century portrait of chaste love – a love based on mutual respect and designed to enhance the moral standing of both parties, and celebrate their union as a shared, blameless endeavour.

He had, as it happens, an available, socially recognisable 'self-fashioned' context nearby for such a public affirmation of the possibility of chaste relations between an unmarried man and woman. Huygens's version of his 'love' for Dorothea, as conveyed in the poems I have referred to, matches closely the fashioned version of male–female friendship as intellectually uplifting and life-enhancing, which he and others had carefully constructed and circulated within a group of artistically and musically gifted young men and women centred on The Hague. These fashionings formed the public personae of the members of the so-called 'Muiden circle' or salon, led by Huygens's close friend and literary sparring-partner. In the constructed scenario, they were supposed to have met regularly (though more recent scholarship supports the view that this too was a literary construct).[7] The central figure was the poet P. C. Hooft, whose official residence was the Muiden Castle. The idea of regular meetings may have been a fiction, but Hooft, Huygens, Joost van den Vondel and the sisters Anna Roemers Visscher

6 I have found no evidence for the details of the vows and rings exchanged by Constantijn and Dorothea, followed by her spurning him and turning to another, apart from the devices in this poem.

7 See L. Strengholt, 'Over de Muiderkring', in *Cultuurfeschiedenis in de Nederlanden van de Renaissance naar de Romantiek. Liber amicorum J. Andriessen S. J., A. Keersmaekers, P. Lenders S. J.* (Leuven: Amersfoort, 1986), pp. 265–70; reprinted in L. Strengholt, *Een Lezer aan het Woord: Studies van L. Strenghold over zeventiende-eeuwse Nederlandse Letterkunde* (Munster: Nodus Publikationem, 1998), pp. 75–88.

and Maria Tesselschade Visscher did together form an epistolary network, exchanging intellectual letters, poems and compliments.

Literary historians used to be content, by and large, to accept at face value the heavily sanitised self-presentation of intellectual and musical 'conversation' in salon circles generated by those like Huygens who frequented them, just as they have accepted the correspondingly tidied-up version of what happened between Constantijn and Dorothea, and the secondary literature is littered with references to the individuals in question as if they belonged to some kind of intellectual salon. In fact, no such salon existed, and the pretence of a kind of 'circle' may be viewed as a construct designed to legitimate conversation (fraternisation) between the talented of both sexes, which might otherwise have been judged indecorous. One might almost say that the social convenience of the 'Muiderkring' as a context within which highly educated, marriage-able young men and women could mingle with propriety has provided critics with an alibi for Constantijn Huygens's perhaps less-than-laud-able youthful behaviour towards his first sweetheart.

Nothing could show more apparently secure propriety, then, than the picture generally painted of relations between the talented poet, painter and glass-engraver Anna Roemers Visscher and her sister Maria Tesselschade Visscher, say, and men like Hooft and Huygens. The surviving Latin letters exchanged between them testify to the elevated nature of the relationships. However, in spite of the temptation to celebrate such an early example of gender equality, it does not take much to cross the dividing line between decorous participation and unseemliness, which was perilously narrow at the time. At the beginning of 1624, for instance, one of the most renowned of the female members of the circle, Anna Roemers Visscher, 'fell in love' and married at the age of forty. In a letter to Constantijn that spring, thirty-some-thing Dorothea van Dorp did not mince her words about how ridiculous she considered Anna's behaviour:

> Anna Roemers is here with her husband. Madame Dimmers has seen her. She shows her husband off as if she were a lovesick young girl. And she's pregnant already – the silly woman! I shall not arrange to see her. I feel sick when I see such an old carcass behaving so idiotically.[8]

8 'Anna Rommers is hier met haren man. Joffrou Dimmers heeft haer gesien. Sy is soo versiert met den man als ofse een jonghe malote waer. Al bevrucht – de siekelijcke vrou! Ick en sal haer niet verwachten om te sien. Ick sou qualijck worden om sulken ouwen crijing soo mal te sien.' Worp, nr. 242, but last sentence missing, presumably omitted as offensive. Cited

In spite of her celebrated talents, then, as soon as Anna Roemers leaves the rarified world of 'art' and becomes emotionally entangled in the 'real' world, her pretended respectability and dignity as a fully participating artistic figure, alongside virtuosi men like Huygens and Hooft, falls away from her. She is in fact nothing more than another stupid woman (by implication, of rather inferior social status), whose company is to be avoided rather than eagerly sought after.[9] In the present context, it is obviously striking that Dorothea van Dorp herself is here prepared to endorse the social vilification of an artistically active and talented woman, as soon as she joins the ranks of common-or-garden wives. The suggestion in this letter is supposed to be, I think, that, as a couple, Dorothea and Constantijn are above such humdrum versions of male–female liaisons.

***

To strip away such surface convention and to explore the Constantijn–Dorothea relationship a little further here, I propose to look at a selection of the surviving letters closely connected with it, to try to excavate a rather more subtle version of their 'friendship' as it is fashioned by epistolary means in the public domain. These are six letters from Constantijn to Dorothea in French (Worp, numbers 80, 84, 177, 310, 311, 342), and six letters from Dorothea to Constantijn in Dutch (Worp, numbers 222, 234, 237, 242, 243, 248).[10] These last were clearly never meant for public circulation, and are, at points, almost alarmingly frank – it is from one of these that I took the passage just quoted about the recently married Anna Roemers Visscher. I shall also

---

from J. A. Alberdingk Thijm, 'Constantin Huygens en de familie van Dorp', *De Dietsche Warande* 6 (1864), 465–89; 485. See also J. A. Worp, *De Dietsche Warande* (1892), 335–44 and 451–60.

9   The same thing had happened a year earlier, when Anna's even more talented and celebrated sister, Maria Tesselschade Visscher, found herself a husband. To support the argument of the present article, one could indeed look in detail at Huygens's epistolary exchanges with Maria Tesselschade Visscher. These are sustainedly highly wrought in their compliments and admiration. Every epistolary convention is employed (including use of Latin to elevate the style) to ensure the decorum of the exchange. Yet in letters to his friend Hooft, Huygens was quite capable of down-to-earth comment on her behaviour – see, for example, his comments to Hooft following her marriage in 1623 (Worp, nr. 216). When the outstanding musician Utricia Ogle married William Swann, Huygens went to elaborate lengths to 'adopt' the husband as well as the wife – something he appears to be recommending to Dorothea van Dorp (that she marry someone congenial to him, so that they can continue their virtuous friendship).

10   Transcriptions of all of these letters can be found in Appendix V. For modern Dutch translations of four of them, see M. B. Smits-Velidt and M. S. Bakker, *In een web van vriendschap: Brieven van vrouwen aan mannen uit de gouden eeuw* (Amsterdam: Querido, 1999), pp. 26–34.

examine two draft letters from Dorothea to the musically accomplished London society hostess, Lady Mary Killigrew, in English.

The first of Constantijn's extant letters to Dorothea, in elegantly poised French, dated 18 May 1620, while Constantijn was on his second diplomatic trip, this time to Venice, begins with what at first sight reads as a declaration of undying love, in terms which convey the flavour of their relationship as he chooses to represent it:

> Little song.[11] I find myself separated from you by a good many days. But I assure you from deep within my heart that you remain perpetually beloved, ranking among those whom God and nature oblige me to honour as well as to love. I take enormous pleasure in recalling your friendship [amitié] – how I wish I were able adequately to begin to express how deeply I feel about it. Circumstances, however, do not allow me to indulge myself at the moment.[12]

At this point, the letter swerves away, without warning, from what reads thus far convincingly as a heartfelt expression of intense feeling for the absent beloved, articulating the love Constantijn feels for Dorothea and his sadness at their separation. Constantijn now adopts instead a high moral tone, which transforms and generalises Dorothea's loving influence on himself into a benign, morally advisory role as guide and muse to his close family:

> Rather [than continuing to express my affection], let me express desire that those closest to me can, in my absence, derive contentment and profit. That is, my good sisters, who I recommend to you, and beg you to be prepared to serve as a salutary example to them, so that they together can continue that honest friendship that I can boast to have maintained for several years with you. I hope that they can derive from you that profit which I would desire you to have gained from my conversation [company]. Take their hand on the pathway towards Godfearingness, which is the

---

11 A number of scholars have tried to find plausible origins for the fact that Dorothea and Constantijn address one other as 'Song', and that sometimes he calls her 'Songetgen' [little Song]. Like all pet names, it is unlikely that we will ever actually get to the bottom of this identical usage of the English word for a melody. I would simply point out that a vocal duet involves two 'singers', each of whom contributes to the achieved harmony which is the 'song'. This is at least as good a reason for their pet-name usage as any other that has been offered.

12 Worp, nr. 80; Appendix V.

source of all virtue, and I can guarantee that you will find that they have emerged from an apprenticeship to two honest and supportive parents, who have planted within them only healthy plants, which will grow some day into saintly and salutary fruits.[13]

Modulated in this fashion, Huygens can now return to his intense scrutiny of Dorothea herself. She has by now been safely elevated to the status of a moral beacon to his sisters, and he addresses her in a tone or register more appropriate to a treatise on conduct than a familiar letter to a sweetheart:

> I do not touch upon the care you must take for yourself, for you know that yourself. In a word, do me the honour of remembering from time to time those exhortations towards gravity and modesty with which I so often assailed your ears. If the most well advised do not conform to these instructions, may my advice be forever out of credit with you. For, *Thehen*, God knows that I attend with a good heart to the advancing of your good reputation, to help you to render it unassailable by any kind of calumny. I am your sincere friend, and thus I speak bluntly to you. If this displeases you, you had better warn me. Here are ill-stitched offerings which I pour out in all haste towards midnight, but the pleasure in speaking to you distracts me from all else.[14]

Having completed his Polonius-like instructions to Dorothea on her proper behaviour in his absence, in the final section of the letter Huygens the lover returns to the lover's conventional concerns – though still in highly contrived fashion. He expresses his anxiety that his frequent, extended absences from The Hague may lead her to turn to another, in which case, he will be reduced to continuing his loving friendship with her as a visitor to her marital home:

> *Kint* [little one], never ever distance yourself from me, and please let it be that I find no change in your heart because of these few months of separation. It is that alone [your heart] which I claim for myself. Dispose of the rest as befits the mistress of the house, I lay no claim to it. But still, if perhaps in my absence the

13   Ibid.
14   Ibid.

desire takes you to attach yourself to somebody else, I beg you to choose someone in tune with myself, and to govern yourself so as to please a little he who lays claim to continuing an immortal friendship with you, even after the day which will see you once and for all given to a husband. For, *Thehe*, it will give me the greatest of pleasure to be able to find you in your household if the head of it is qualified in the ways I would wish for you. I hand over everything to your discretion and will accept the unfortunate outcome of whatever happens.[15]

The highly wrought conventionality of this letter (and those that follow) ought not to surprise us. We should remember that any letter Huygens sent to Dorothea through official channels would be expected to be shown to her parents, and indeed, passed around her familiar circle – in at least one of his letters, Constantijn instructs Dorothea to show her own letter to another member of their circle to whom he owes a letter, but to whom he has not as yet had time to write:

Thank Mad[ame] Trello for the delightful letter she did me the honour of writing to me. I take this as firm assurance of her affection towards me, on the grounds that a single word is worth more than ten thoughts. To excuse me from having failed to reply to her, just show her this word, so that she can judge how precious my leisure moments are to me, and how few of them I have.[16]

In fact, the physical appearance of these letters from Constantijn to Dorothea as they survive in the Huygen archives makes the semi-public nature of these letters explicit. The letter just quoted has been carefully folded and sealed with Constantijn's seal, but it carries no address, which implies that it was enclosed within another, addressed letter. Of the remaining letters, one carries on its outside page an address 'A Madamoiselle Dorothee Van Dorps/A La Haye' and Constantijn's seal, but is followed by a blank sheet, which again carries the remains of Huygens's seal and the address of the relatives with whom she was at this point staying in Amsterdam. Thus the letter, although private to Dorothea, will have been received by her relatives, and opened by them, thus allowing them to inquire about the contents of her letter.

15   Ibid.
16   Worp, nr. 84, 18 June 1620.

Even more strikingly, the two letters Huygens sent to Dorothea in 1626, shortly after she had learned that he was to marry Susanna van Baerle, appear to have been sent together – the sheets of paper and handwriting are strikingly alike – and the outer blank page of the second of these again bears the address of Dorothea's relations in Antwerp plus Constantijn's seal. So in this case, the family were the first to see the letters themselves, which are not made private to Dorothea.[17]

Subsequent letters oscillate in precisely the same manner between expressions of intense feeling, testifying to strong emotional commitment, and studied avowals of morally uplifting bonds between Huygens and the entire Dorp family – represented as beacons of propriety and seriousness. This is, in my view, a classic piece of conscious self-fashioning, in which the subject strenuously re-organises his sentimental environment to his own best advantage, by adopting and using adeptly conventions agreed on by the community in which he operates.

It hardly needs saying that the idea of Dorothea as a muse to the Huygens family is not a version of the Huygens–Dorp family relations which is to be found anywhere else in the historical account – Dorothea, indeed, subsequently complains to Constantijn of his family's coldness towards her. And of course, we are only glimpsing the epistolary relationship here being constructed. The surviving letters I am considering are only a small sample of the many letters being exchanged between Constantijn and Dorothea in the period 1620 to 1624. In a letter of 12 May 1624, for instance, Dorothea writes to Constantijn that 'if I had had the opportunity to write to you as often as I wished, you would have a letter a week from me. I have, in the time you have been away, received 4 letters, and this is the fourth.'[18] The tone of Constantijn's letters is such, though, that there is no reason to think that missing letters from this period would differ in significant ways from those that have survived.

Dorothea's letters in Dutch to Constantijn, by contrast, are in an entirely different register. They are racy, colloquial, full of local gossip, and charmingly direct. Of course, familiar Dutch necessarily has a different 'feel' to it from court French. Still, Dorothea's letters are liberally strewn with gossip and scandal of a kind, and in a tone of voice which is surely only intended for Constantijn (remember

---

17   Den Haag, Kon. Bibl., Hs. KA XLIX-1. The letters are at ff. 349–61.
18   'Had ick soo dickmaels gelegenthijt om te schrijven als lust, ghij hadt alle weeck eenen brief van mijn. Ick heb, soo lang all ghij wech geweest hebt, 4 briefen behadt, en dit is oock den vierden' (Worp, nr. 237).

those barbed remarks about Anna Roemers Visscher). To take their full implications for an evaluation of the fashioned version of their friendship on show in Constantijn's letters, however, it is necessary to introduce here some background information concerning Constantijn's circumstances on his second and third periods of residence in London, which is the setting for many of Dorothea's most pointed epistolary exchanges.

**

On his second stay in England in 1622, Constantijn Huygens struck up a lasting friendship with the well-connected, welcoming Killigrew family, who were close neighbours to his diplomatic lodgings in London. Theirs was a bustling, vibrant, artistic household, with parents and at least eight children (the eldest about seventeen), all of whom participated in well-attended musical soirées. A talented lutenist and singer himself, Constantijn acknowledged in later life that he had been deeply influenced by the Killigrews and the excitement of their intoxicating intellectual milieu. His enthusiasm betrays perhaps the 'provincial' Dutchman's fascination with the 'high' metropolitan atmosphere. There, alongside the royalty and nobility who regularly visited to be entertained – and as well as the music – he first encountered the celebrated English poets John Donne and Ben Jonson, and rubbed shoulders with those we would call 'scientists' like the Lord Chancellor Sir Francis Bacon, and the inventor and illusionist Cornelius Drebbel.[19]

Presiding over this glamorous household was Lady Mary Killigrew, later to become 'Lady Stafford' after her remarriage to Sir Thomas Stafford, gentleman-usher to Queen Henrietta Maria, following the death of her first husband Sir Robert Killigrew in 1633.[20] Although in later life Constantijn Huygens would insist that his infatuation with the Killigrews had extended to the entire family, his surviving correspondence, and his Latin poetic autobiography, make it clear that he was particularly taken with (and emotionally involved with) Lady Mary,

19 See A. G. H. Bachrach, *Sir Constantijn Huygens and some Trends in the Literature and Art of Seventeenth Century England and Holland* (Thesis submitted for the Degree of DPhil in the University of Oxford, 1951). I am extremely grateful to Dr Ad Leerintveld of the Koninklijke Bibliotheek for bringing this thesis to my attention.

20 The change in name has meant that her continuing friendship with Huygens gets overlooked as he begins to correspond with 'Lady Stafford' rather than 'Lady Killigrew'. Inge Broekman tells me that there exists a reference to Huygens's having owned a portrait of Mary Killigrew, which hung in his private art collection (I. Broekman, personal communication, 28 November 2008).

with her 'snow-white throat' and 'divine voice' (as he later recalled them). At the time at which he first knew her, Lady Killigrew was referred to in London as 'the young, French' Lady Killigrew (implying a certain moral laxity, one gathers). She appears to have been pregnant for most of Huygens's time in London (her last two children were born in 1622 and 1623), so I am not suggesting that this was more than a flirtation. On the other hand, the decorum of their relationship was surely questionable. Even late in life, Huygens would remember his hostess with particular passionate fervour. Tellingly, that same autobiographical poem which refers to Lady Killigrew's physical attractiveness and musical brilliance contains no mention of Dorothea whatsoever.[21]

In March 1623, Dorothea wrote two letters in English to Lady Killigrew – or at least, that is when the letters were drafted, according to the dates at the bottom of the manuscripts preserved among the KB Huygens letters. To be more precise: at the bottom of the first letter has been written 'Hague, this [blank] of March 1623', indicating that the date is to be filled in later; the second letter carries no date, but at the top, in a later hand, is written '1623 perhaps' ('for[si]tan'). Both letters carry the superscription, 'For m[adam]e dor[othea] van dorp for the Lady Killigrew'.

The first letter is a kind of self-introduction, offering a small gift and dedicated service to Mary Killigrew, based on Constantijn Huygens's glowing recommendation of her virtues. It might be intended to commence a negotiation concerning some kind of position for Dorothea in the Killigrew household (elsewhere in her letters Dorothea makes it clear that she is working hard on her English: 'you know why', she says to Constantijn):

> Madame: The testimonies my friend S[ir] Constantin Huygens hath giuen me heretofore by his letters of y[our] Lad[yships] most rare and singular qualities, are so great and so manie, that even afore I saw him I found myselfe short of wordes in mine owne language, by w[hich] I could haue giuen y[our] Lad[yship] the thankes I owed y[ou] for esteeming me worth the offring of y[our] special loue and friendshippe; the remembrance of w[hich]

21 '... solam, / Killigraea domus, si te cito, dixero multas. / ... Tota domus concentus erat: pulcherrima mater, / Mater (adhuc stupeo) duodenae prolis, ab illo / Gutture tam niveo, tam nil mortale sonanti / Quam coeleste Melos Citharae sociabat, et ipso / Threïcio (dicas) animatis pollice chordis!' Constantijn Huygens, *Mijn leven verteld aan mijn kinderen in twee boeken*. Ingeleid, bezorgd, vertaald en van commentaar voorzien door Frans R. E. Blom, Amsterdam 2003, 2 vols. Sermonum inter libros. Lib. II, 150–87, Part. 1, pp. 124–6, Part 2, pp. 216–73.

kindnesse hauing since beene renewed to me by the said my friend in report of y[our] deserts hath putt me backe from expressing in this forreine language what in my owne I was not able to do before. Yet notwithstanding choosing rather to haue my ignorance discouered then my unthankfullnesse suspected, I resolued to send y[our] Lad[yship] these lines for to accompanie these poore trifles, upon w[hich] (though in their value most like their giuer) I will humble beseech y[our] Lad[yship] to bestow the honour of y[our] wearing, and sometimes at y[our] best leasure remember by them that in Holland liueth. Madam; Y[our] Lad[yships] humble and most loueing seruant D. v. D.[22]

The second letter, while still formal, is less conventional in its phrasing and sentiments. It vividly conveys Dorothea's strong reaction to what appears to have been a letter of congratulation of some kind from Lady Killigrew, probably a suggestion that Dorothea was not 'attached', or promised in marriage to Constantijn. Such an imputation might have been entirely innocent – part of Lady's Killigrew's inquiries as to whether Dorothea was free to come to England, say. But the clarification of the fact that she was entirely unattached, could, of course, only have come from Constantijn, and would have been a convenient fiction if he wished to indicate his own freedom from commitment at home in order to flirt with Mary Killigrew. Either way, Dorothea took it to mean that Constantijn had declared that their past attachment to one another was at an end:

Madame: I do not know what impressions my friend hath bene about to giue y[our] Lad[yship] concerning I cannot tell what change of the condition of my life: but guessing at it by y[our] Lad[yships] answeres, I dare say he doth long to see thinges brought to such an ende as he hath bene pleased to imagine, afore nor I nor anie liuing sowle thought of it. For the truth is, I do liue quietlie in the same estate, he left me and found me at his going and coming from England: neither do I see anie reason why I should wish to alter it. Howbeit, what kind of life so euer one day or other God shall be pleased to call me unto, he needeth not to feare for a while. The willing friendshipp I contracted w[ith] him euen almost from his childhood is such as no alteration will be able to alter it no, not this very unciuill doing of his. No more then

22   Den Haag, Kon. Bibl., Hs. KA XLVIII, f. 56.

the affection I vowed to the seruice of y[our] Lad[yship] in regard of w[hich] I am bold to call my selfe for ever Madame y[our] Lad[yships] Humble and most aff[ectionate] seruant, D.[23]

What is at first sight remarkable is that not just the first, but also the second of these letters is in Constantijn Huygens's unmistakeable handwriting (which explains the 'For m[adame] dor[othea] van dorp for the Lady Killigrew' – these are drafts for her use). They are also, to anyone who has worked with his English letters, rather obviously entirely drafted by him (they are, as they say, in his 'voice'). Both preserve clear signs of having been folded in the manner of a standard letter of the time, implying (since they lack addresses) that they were sent as enclosures, presumably to Dorothea, for copying in her own hand.[24]

That this should be so in the case of the first letter is perhaps not surprising. Huygens is assisting Dorothea in a patronage bid, and therefore provides her with the language, style and register appropriate to such a formal approach. The same cannot be said of the second letter. It voices sentiments of indignation against Constantijn – the very person drafting the letter (though, because of the complexity of its language and syntax Dorothea, with her limited English, could perhaps not follow precisely what was being said).

***

Here we have a positively soap-opera scenario, perhaps engineered by a mischievous Lady Killigrew, which Constantijn now has to rectify, to preserve his reputation, not to mention those of his London hostess and his 'fiancée' in The Hague.

Dorothea van Dorp makes it quite clear that she considers the friendship which has developed between Constantijn and Lady Mary (twelve years older than him, attractive and vivacious, mother of a brood of adorable children), during the fourteen-month Dutch Embassy to London of 1622–3, to be by no means innocent, and is signalling that

23 Den Haag, Kon. Bibl., Hs. KA XLVIII, f. 57. These letters have been transcribed in R. L. Colie, 'Some Thankfulnesse to Constantine'. A Study of English Influence upon the Early Works of Constantijn Huygens (The Hague: Martinus Nijhoff, 1956), pp. 27–8.

24 It was a graduate student from Utrecht University, David van der Linden, participating in a Masterclass led by myself for the Huizinga Institute, in the KB library in November 2008, who pointed out the folds (but no address) which showed not only that these drafts had been sent inside another letter, but also that the second one had been kept folded for some time (as the dirt-marks on its outer side show). I am extremely grateful to David for this important insight into the fortunes of these two curious missives.

Lady Killigrew is treading on her sentimental toes. We have evidence from Dorothea's own letters (in Dutch) that this was indeed so. In May 1624, when Constantijn returned for some months to London, following the death of his father in February of that year, Dorothea's letters refer pointedly to the competition between herself and Lady Killigrew.[25] When Lady Killigrew sends her the gift of a bracelet, Dorothea retorts with emotion: 'I deserve this and more for my lending her so long what I can do without so badly.' 'I shall also have my picture dispatched to her', she goes on.[26]

When Dorothea responds with her own reciprocal gift for Lady Killigrew (as convention and good manners requires), her barbed comment to Constantijn makes her feelings about the situation very clear:

> I am sending you the amber bracelet for Lady Killigrew. I am pleased that she desires something from me. It and all that I have in the world are hers to command. She will do it the greatest honour by wearing it, and will oblige me by doing so. Tell her this comes from someone who is her servant more than anyone has ever been, all her lovers notwithstanding. . . . Please send my respects to her gracious goodness. Tell her she may indeed believe I love her, because I am prepared to let her share the same joy as myself, and am willing to renounce my own pleasure for her sake. Do tell her so. Please do not forget the little ring she promised me.[27]

In a particularly personal postscript, Dorothea asks Huygens to secure for her some additional cornelian beads for her own bracelet – the one, presumably, that Lady Killigrew has sent her – if he can do so easily. The bracelet is too small to go around her wrist. There can be no doubting the strength of feeling here, nor the sense of ownership Dorothea feels entitled to express in an intimate letter to Constantijn.

So what are we to make of the two letters from Dorothea to Lady Killigrew 'ghosted' by Constantijn Huygens? My suggestion is that here we see Huygens's self-fashioning fully at work – extending, indeed, beyond the contours of his own body to include that of his 'friend' Dorothea.

---

25 Huygens finally returned to The Hague on 5 July 1624 (see 'reversus' against this date in *Dagboek*, p. 10).

26 Bachrach, *Sir Constantijn Huygens*, p. 223.

27 Worp, nr. 242; Appendix V.

First, Constantijn orchestrates – literally ventriloquises – the giving of token gifts to his English hostess by Dorothea, carefully crafting the approach as the courtly gesture, or 'paying court' it is intended to be. Perhaps he salves his conscience by explicitly involving Dorothea in his London life, perhaps he persuades himself that he is thereby offering her a golden opportunity to 'come up' in the world, by putting her in a position to enter Lady Killigrew's household herself. Eager to please, as always, Dorothea obliges by transcribing his letter creating her as a gracious English courtier, and ascribing it to herself.

Lady Killigrew evidently replied (as she would be required to do out of pure *politesse*), and in doing so implied that she had been informed that Dorothea was not in any way attached to Constantijn, was, indeed, spoken for elsewhere. Now Constantijn is required to repair the damage done at both ends of his carefully engineered correspondence between rivals for his affection. The result is the second letter. Once again the genuinely aggrieved Dorothea obligingly goes along with the fiction that this had been, at worst, a misunderstanding. But she makes it extremely clear that whatever claims she has on Constantijn persist:

> I dare say he doth long to see thinges brought to such an ende as he hath bene pleased to imagine, afore nor I nor anie liuing sowle thought of it. [But] the truth is, I do liue quietlie in the same estate, he left me and found me at his going and coming from England: neither do I see anie reason why I should wish to alter it. . . . The willing friendshipp I contracted w[ith] him euen almost from his childhood is such as no alteration will be able to alter it no, not this very unciuill doing of his.

***

If this seems a far-fetched interpretation (it is, by the way, the only one I am satisfied by which makes sense of all the data), let us turn, finally, to the last letters we have that Constantijn sent to Dorothea, in 1626. By this time, as numerous poems to 'sterre' or Susanna van Baerle, written during the same period, make clear, Constantijn had committed himself to the woman who would become his wife in April 1627.

In April 1626, Constantijn wrote two letters to Dorothea, dated close together, or perhaps even on the same day. They are written in response to a report (received by Huygens via her brother, perhaps with strong accompanying protest) that there has been a violent altercation in the Huygens household, between Dorothea's step-mother and Constantijn's mother. He has no idea what the cause of the to-do is, he claims, but if it is supposed to have anything to do with him, he is blameless:

> I was not present at this discussion that Madame van Dorp had with my mother, and which she has no doubt told you all about – since, unkindly, it erupted in front of those who have nothing to do. But if she continues to lay the blame on me, as I have learned indirectly she is trying to do, I will find myself finally forced to open my books [i.e. show my correspondence] publicly. I can assure her that when I do so she will read there her own confusion, and my sincere affection towards her and all her family. Only someone truly ungrateful could claim the contrary.[28]

Here the care Huygens had taken with those fashioned letters we looked at earlier provides him with precisely the moral 'cover' needed at the moment when he discards the passionate 'friendship' with Dorothea in favour of a decorous marital union with Susanna van Baerle. Let anyone who chooses read his letters to Dorothea, and they will find them beyond reproach, he writes. That, after all, was exactly how they were contrived in the first place – to be able to be read in two senses, depending on the inclination of the reader to find passion or chastity in their language and expression.[29]

Constantijn's second letter reiterates to Dorothea – who has apparently fallen gravely ill in the aftermath of the announcement of his engagement to Susanna – that she should pay no heed to the tittle-tattle of 'friends' who consider her, Dorothea, to have been spurned, and her reputation damaged:

> At the moment, in my view, you are taking the gossip too seriously, and the discontent your friends have conceived towards you cannot be rebutted to your advantage, as I promise myself you will be able to do once you can defend yourself to them face to face. I see difficulties arising here from the fact that people never

---

28 Worp, nr. 310; Appendix V.
29 As early as 1620, on his embassy to Venice, as noted above, Constantijn suggests to Dorothea that she might like to show the letter he has written to her to 'Madame de Trello' (Dorothea's step-mother's sister, who formed part of their intellectual and musical circle), in lieu of his replying to a letter from her himself. In other words, he writes on the assumption that his letters will be shown to others besides the recipient (as indeed do letter-writers generally in this period).

understand the way things are in depth, and others do not want to do so. As for myself, I have always had reserves of strength which at worst guarantee me against all calumny. But I am upset to see the disorder among our friends, and would be pleased if you would take the time to explain things to them, instead of letting others do so, thereby making things seem worse than they really are.[30]

In spite of these protestations, Dorothea herself was clearly not mollified, even if Constantijn could absolve himself from blame by referring to those dozens of carefully contrived letters he had sent her over the preceding five or more years. Huygens's final letter to her in this sequence acknowledges this to be the case. On the eve of his marriage, he writes to tell her that he has been successful in securing the position of Admiral-lieutenant for her brother Philips – an achievement he apparently hopes will mend bridges between himself and the van Dorp family. He does not, however, hold out much hope that this will appease Dorothea:

> You have so misunderstood my intentions, that it seems to me that nothing I do now can cause you any less offence. I mean to say that you wear the importunity of my behaviour like a scar.[31]

***

So much for the scholarly view that Dorothea herself had jilted Constantijn for another while he was away, ten years earlier. Which brings me to my conclusion. What is surprising here is not the story I have just narrated, which resembles many others, then and now, in which the construction being placed on a relationship differs according to which of the parties concerned is describing it. No, what comes as a surprise is the tacit agreement shared among almost all serious scholars of Constantijn Huygens that there had been nothing disreputable or to be reproached in his behaviour towards her – that any fault lay on her side. The fiction extends to the often repeated information that Dorothea 'went off and married someone else' – in fact, she never married. It is as if the scholarly community would rather abandon its customary critical scruples, and agree to turn a blind eye to the youthful behaviour of Holland's greatest virtuoso.

And please understand, I am not, here, taking sides. Who is to say whose version of the love between Constantijn and Dorothea was

---

30   Worp, nr. 311; Appendix V.
31   Worp, nr. 343; Appendix V.

the more accurate, not to mention the most appropriate? But as we reflect upon the textual self-fashioning of that great connoisseur and musical virtuoso, cultural advisor to princes, and pre-eminent Dutch statesman, Sir Constantijn Huygens, here, surely, is a striking example of his early ability to fashion himself to his future destiny, to which scholars heretofore should have given serious and sustained attention. At least let us hope that in future they will take more care to give letters like these in the Huygens corpus their full critical attention, thereby allowing them to see beyond the surface conventions which we now understand fashioned the very public presence of this extraordinary figure.

6

The Afterlife of Homo Ludens: From Johan Huizinga to Natalie Zemon Davis and Beyond

It was not my object to define the place of play among all other manifestations of culture, but rather to ascertain how far culture itself bears the character of play. (Johan Huizinga, *Homo Ludens*, Foreword)

For us *Homo ludens* is a more complex person ... and modern theoreticians have tried to sort out his games as they appear and are used in different cultures. (Natalie Zemon Davis, 'The reasons of misrule: Youth groups and charivaris in sixteenth-century France', *Past & Present* 50 [1971], 48–9)

This is an essay about the continuing importance, for the English-speaking world, of Johan Huizinga's innovative approach to cultural history, especially as articulated in his often cited (but rather less often read) work, *Homo Ludens* (first published in Dutch in 1938, first English translation 1949, first generally available edition 1955).[1]

Huizinga is a master story-teller, whose material is drawn from the everyday detail, literature and poetry of the late middle ages, and who weaves documented incident and event into a richly varied tapestry of the forms of 'life, art and thought' of ordinary people in France and Holland in the fourteenth and fifteenth centuries.

Here is how he captures the way in which, in the fifteenth century, the 'cruel reality' of inevitable physical suffering and violent death was compensated for by the use of elaborate rituals and exaggerated

---

1   There appears to have been a Routledge and Kegan Paul hardback edition, based on the German text of *Homo Ludens*, published c. 1949. All subsequent commentators, however, refer to the Beacon Press edition, first published in 1955.

displays of public grief. These, according to Huizinga, 'made life an art', transforming grim experience to make it tolerable: 'The cultural value of ritualised mourning,' he writes, 'is that it gives grief its form and rhythm. It transfers actual life to the sphere of the drama. Mourning at the court of France or of Burgundy dramatised the effects of grief.'

The idea which today we can understand to be central to Huizinga's *Homo Ludens* is a richly suggestive methodological one. If we regard systematic (public and private) forms of human behaviour as potentially rule-governed 'games', then the strategies used within communities by 'players' to modify, ironise or subvert the rules of the game can be scrutinised by the cultural historian for their capacity to illuminate the way social structures inform and shape the behaviour of individuals.[2]

> Real civilization [writes Huizinga] cannot exist in the absence of a play-element, for civilization presupposes limitation and mastery of the self, the ability not to confuse its own tendencies with the ultimate and highest goal, but to understand that it is enclosed within certain bounds freely accepted. Civilization will, in a sense, always be played according to certain rules.[3]

And he adds a final point, to which we will return: 'True civilization will always demand fair play. Fair play is nothing less than good faith expressed in play terms. Hence the cheat or the spoil-sport shatters civilization itself.'

My proposition, that Huizinga continues to exert significant current influence, may come as a surprise to you. Among those writing about Huizinga, particularly in the Netherlands, starting shortly after his death in 1945, there seems to have been a measure of agreement that in spite of his unique brilliance and originality, he ultimately failed to generate a significant 'movement', or to enter the historiographical mainstream.[4]

---

2 Since I drafted this essay, I have become aware of the fact that John von Neumann and Oskar Morganstern's *Theory of Games and Economic Behavior*, published in 1944 by Princeton University Press, incorporated work developed in an article published by von Neumann in 1928, 'Zur Theorie der Gesellschaftsspiele'. In other words, mathematical game theory was developing over precisely the same period as Huizinga's history-based version of the same idea – that all human behaviour could usefully be treated as varieties of 'game', in which individual players had a significant measure of autonomy and reciprocity in decision-making towards a solution or outcome.

3 Huizinga, *Homo Ludens* (English translation, Boston, Mass.: Beacon Press, 1955), p. 211.

4 See, for example, P. Geyl, 'Huizinga as accuser of his Age', *History and Theory* 2 (1963), 231–62; J. Katz, 'A reply to J. Huizinga on the form and function of history', *Journal of the History of Ideas*, 5 (1944), 369–73.

To be sure, since the 1980s, scholars such as Frank Ankersmit, Wessel Krul, Anton van der Lem and Willem Otterspeer have done much to bring Huizinga once again to the forefront of historiographical debate in the Netherlands, and Huizinga lends his name to a number of academic institutions and buildings. But I intend to show here that in the interval between the immediately-post-Second-World-War generation (critics like Pieter Geyl) and theirs, English-language development of Huizinga's seminal ideas had been going on apace, and had already contributed strongly to fundamentally new fields of cultural studies.

I shall suggest that if we trace the footprints of Huizinga's work with care through works plainly influenced by him, we will find that his brilliant formulation of the methodological function of play as a distinctive strategy for understanding and analysing the past (as proposed in *Homo Ludens*) has indelibly marked the thinking of innovative cultural historians in Britain and North America down to the present day. I shall maintain, indeed, that landmark works by ground-breaking cultural historians – specifically Natalie Zemon Davis's *Return of Martin Guerre* and Stephen Greenblatt's *Renaissance Self-Fashioning*, two pivotal works for the emergence of today's thriving schools of cultural history and literary historicism – stand in direct line of descent methodologically from historically revelatory moves made by Johan Huizinga in *The Waning of the Middle Ages*, and above all, in *Homo Ludens*.

My starting point is 1972 – the centenary of Huizinga's birth – when a fresh wave of interest in *Homo Ludens* coincided in a particularly productive way with emerging new fields in cultural history, social anthropology and literary text studies. Reading *Homo Ludens* gave the proponents and practitioners in these fields an essential plank for the epistemological platform shared across their new academic movements, and Huizinga's approach has provided a crucial (if often unacknow-ledged) justification for their work ever since.

I single out one person in particular who seems to have helped facilitate the largely unremarked dissemination of Huizinga's work (particularly that on 'play') across English-language Renaissance cultural studies – someone whose ability to bridge the gap between Huizinga's immediately post-war world in the Netherlands and the academy in post-war North America actively enabled the absorption of his work into the tissue of emerging cultural studies there. This figure is Rosalie L. Colie, best known in the English-speaking world for her fascinating study of the playful use of language in Renaissance thought, *Paradoxia*

Epidemica,[5] and in the Netherlands for her extraordinarily perceptive study of the seventeenth-century Anglophile polymath, Sir Constantijn Huygens ('*Some Thankfulnesse to Constantine*').[6] Colie was comfortable with the Dutch language, and it was in no small part through her efforts that Huizinga's work was brought directly to the attention of key figures in the English-speaking intellectual world.[7] By her mediation of Huizinga to non-Dutch speakers, some considerable time before most of his work became available in English (or even in the German in which Ernst Gombrich read him), Colie eased his introduction, and focused critical attention on aspects of his work which those concentrating too closely on ideological struggles inside the Dutch academy had perhaps overlooked. Rosalie Colie's career was cut short when she died in a canoeing accident, in her forties, in July 1972.[8]

There are several textual clues in the writings of Colie's contemporaries to support my suggestion that she ought to be considered a key figure in the transmission of Huizinga's ideas. Ernst Gombrich's perceptive article 'Johan Huizinga's *Homo Ludens*', delivered to the Johan Huizinga conference in Groningen in December 1972 (and published a year later) is dedicated: 'To the memory of Rosalie L. Colie (1925–1972)', while the first footnote to Natalie Zemon Davis's seminal 1971 article on the serious significance of the carnivalesque, 'The reasons of misrule: Youth groups and charivaris in sixteenth-century France', contains a similarly direct acknowledgement to her colleague at the University of Toronto, Rosalie Colie: 'I am grateful to colleagues in several fields for suggestions and bibliographical advice, but I want here especially to acknowledge the assistance of Rosalie L. Colie.'[9]

5 *Paradoxia Epidemica* (Princeton: Princeton University Press, 1966).
6 '*Some Thankfulnesse to Constantine*' *A Study of English Influence upon the Early Works of Constantijn Huygens* (The Hague: Martinus Nijhoff, 1956).
7 Throughout her first direct intervention concerning Huizinga ('Johan Huizinga and the task of cultural history' (see n. 10 below), Colie cites Huizinga's individual publications from the *Verzamelde Werken* (ed. L. Brummel et al., 9 vs, Haarlem, 1948–53) in the original Dutch.
8 'Rosalie L. Colie, internationally celebrated for her work in the cultural history of early modern Europe, drowned on July 7, 1972, when her canoe overturned in the Lieutenant River near her home in Old Lyme, Connecticut. Her years were cut unseasonably short, but in them were compressed many lifetimes of creativity, courage, and generosity' (Natalie Zemon Davis obituary, *The American Historical Review* 78 [1973], 757).
9 See E. H. Gombrich, 'Huizinga's *Homo ludens*', in W. R. H. Koops, E. H. Kossmann and G. van der Plaat (eds), *Johan Huizinga 1872–1972* (The Hague, Martinus Nijhoff, 1973), pp. 133–54; 133; N. Z. Davis, 'The reasons of misrule: Youth groups and charivaris in sixteenth-century France', *Past & Present* 50 (1971), 41–75; 133. Davis specifically remembers Colie drawing her attention to an article by Mikhail Bakhtin on Rabelais, but also credits her with all-round discussion of carnival and play: 'I speak of her in a few places in my Passion for History, though there in connection with her friendly support when

Colie's contribution depended on her taking intensely seriously, and interpreting afresh, the key ideas of *Homo Ludens*, in ways that went beyond anything that would have been possible at the time of Huizinga's death, particularly in her important work on metaphysical poetry's 'play' on words, *Paradoxia Epidemica* (1966).

It is Huizinga's ideas, I suggest, as mediated by Colie, that set the direction of travel for the cultural historical and literary movement associated with the phrase 'self-fashioning' – a coinage of Stephen Greenblatt's in 1980, which was embraced by historians such as Natalie Zemon Davis in the early 1980s.

But first a word of clarification is needed, because Colie sometimes gets bundled in with early readers who had reservations about Huizinga's achievements. In 1964, as part of her 'promotion' of Huizinga to the English-speaking academic community, Colie published her own contribution to the on-going, largely Dutch post-war debate concerning Huizinga's version of 'cultural history' in *The American Historical Review*, under the title 'Johan Huizinga and the task of cultural history' – a play on his own article, 'The task of cultural history' ('De taak van cultuur-geschiedenis').[10] Although her intention was clearly to bring Huizinga to the attention of a North American audience, her need to 'deal with' hostile assessments of his work by his contemporaries does get in the way of her primary purpose.

What she tried to do was to justify Huizinga's outlook by setting the man himself in his own cultural historical context – making Huizinga himself, as she puts it, the subject of a cultural historical analysis and contextualisation. Unfortunately, the practical effect was to bring the Dutch-language criticisms of Pieter Geyl, Jan Romein and Menno ter Braak to an English-language audience not well acquainted themselves yet with Huizinga's work. Thereafter, those who wished to emphasise above all the limitations of Huizinga's work were able to cite Colie alongside these others for their dissatisfaction with Huizinga's approach, although the substance of much of their criticism had little to do with its possible applications, and a great deal to do with what were seen as his personal shortcomings faced with the ideological context of the Second World War and Dutch Occupation, in terms

I was a young mother and her telling me about Bakhtin, at the time I gave her the first draft of my charivari paper ("Reasons of misrule") to read. But the whole issue of play, of *Homo Ludens*, was background to our discussions in those days, as were some other writings on play – though I don't know that we talked of Huizinga in detail' (personal communication, 4 October 2010).

10 Rosalie L. Colie, 'Johan Huizinga and the task of cultural history', *The American Historical Review* 69 (1964), 607–30.

of which Huizinga appeared resolutely pessimistic about the state of contemporary civilisation, disinclined to engage with current political reality, and nostalgically yearning for better times in the past.

As a result, the succinct and sharply focused account of the strength of *Homo Ludens* that stands at the heart of Colie's article tends to get overlooked. Colie had written:

> *Homo Ludens* . . . was just what it said it was, a study of the play element in culture. 'Culture' was Oriental, ancient, medieval, and modern history; the 'play element', the games of philosophy, war, law, literature, the arts, as well as play in childhood and in adult life. Out of the phenomena Huizinga constructed a theory, not of games, but of something much more fundamental: a theory of the functions of play, always seen against the ostensibly more serious 'normal' modes of life. . . . *Homo Ludens* is the history neither of playing nor the idea of play. It is a morphological study of play, an interpretation of human behavior based upon comparative examples.[11]

The plea at the end of her article for continued attention to Huizinga's work ('this monument lying athwart the path of [Dutch historians'] profession' as she describes it earlier) is similarly affirmative:

> Huizinga indeed left no school, but he left the testament of his talents. It is up to cultural historians to dispose of his legacy. We may choose to bury our one talent in the ground (which heaven knows, is the easiest thing to do with it), but if we do that, we will find our talent taken from us at the judgment and given to [some] other servant of history who has dared trade with his five talents and come to the judgment with ten [Matthew 25:14–30].[12]

I understand this to mean that Colie believes that it will be thoroughly worthwhile for her generation to invest scholarly effort in developing Huizinga's original idea of play to their own intellectual ends, thereby turning his original investment into a handsome reward for those who come after him.[13]

11 Colie, 'Huizinga and the task of cultural history', p. 614.
12 Colie, 'Huizinga and the task of cultural history', p. 630.
13 Ernst Gombrich too, in his 1972 conference paper on Huizinga dedicated to Colie's memory, attempts a contextualised view of the significance of *Homo Ludens*. Once again, Gombrich acknowledged the influence of that work on his own (he cites his *Meditations on a Hobby Horse* as directly indebted), but he too ends up lamenting Huizinga's failure properly to

In Colie's own important book, *Paradoxia Epidemica*, she makes Huizinga's influence on her approach plainly apparent. Since her theme is the way in which playful use of language and imagery in the Renaissance – from John Donne to Robert Burton – can be explored to uncover a serious problematising of the reality beneath its surface, the indebtedness can be said to underpin her entire enterprise.

***

As I noted, one of those who responded to Colie's enthusiasm for theories of carnival and play was the cultural historian of early modern France, Natalie Zemon Davis. Here is how, in a recent interview, she describes Colie's influence on her own early work:

> When I was still a graduate student and in my early years, I much appreciated the work and friendship of Rosalie Colie (she taught in the English department at the University of Toronto for a time in the late 1960s, but I got to know her in the 1950s). I was much impressed by her interdisciplinary cultural history of the 16th and 17th century and by the way she placed ideas in a broad nexus of communication among scholars and across national boundaries. I loved her book on paradoxes, *Paradoxia Epidemica*.[14]

In a recent personal communication she adds:

> When I think back on that conversation with Rosalie, who liked the 'Reasons of Misrule paper', I see how important she was as a link between Huizinga and me, especially because of her interest in paradox. She was less playful, but she certainly encouraged me to follow the line I was on.[15]

In the 1971 essay, 'Reasons of misrule: youth groups and charivaris in sixteenth-century France' to which she here refers, Natalie Davis picked up and developed the idea of the play-element intrinsic to group

provide a theoretical framework for his importantly suggestive, anecdotal compilations of example of culture as play.

14 Natalie Zemon Davis, interview 2010, http://medievalists.net: http://www.medievalists. net/2008/09/27/interview-with-natalie-zemon-davis/.
    Natalie Davis tells me that until recently she still owned her original copy of *Homo Ludens*, heavily underlined and annotated throughout: 'I still have my much marked up paper-back of *Homo Ludens* from many years ago, which showed me whole new ways to think about the past and to which I feel indebted even when I found my own paths for play' (personal communication, 18 October 2010).

15 Natalie Zemon Davis, personal communication, 21 October 2010.

behaviour in all societies. She argued for the need to take early modern carnivals of 'misrule' – classic examples of 'play' in Huizinga's terms – seriously, as fundamental to our historical understanding of social organisation:

> As for theories of play, I have stressed the rule and rationale in popular festivals and the extent to which they remain in close touch with the realities of community and marriage. These are natural consequences of the carnival licence to deride and the historical nature of festive organizations. It is an exaggeration to view the carnival and misrule as merely a 'safety valve', as merely a primitive, pre-political form of recreation. Bakhtin is closer to the truth in seeing it as present in all cultures. I would say that not only is it present, but that the structure of the carnival form can evolve so that it can act *both to reinforce order and suggest alternatives to the existing order.* [my emphasis][16]

Her subtle repositioning of the historian's attention moves Huizinga's argument beyond where it had taken Colie. For Colie, the attraction of Huizinga's *'serio ludere'* was that it allowed her to take seriously, as key to her linguistic and literary exploration, the plays on words and ideas which typify seventeenth-century poetry and prose in English (the so-called 'metaphysicals').

Natalie Davis took Huizinga's *'serio ludere'* back into social history, and develops its key ideas in much more complex fashion. Instead of a relatively straightforward juxtaposition of paradox or irony with something like 'documented experience', she argues that the act of playing, against the grain of the social order, both serves to acknowledge that regulated order, and offers the potential to modify it:

> What then can we conclude about the character of misrule in the French countryside in the ... sixteenth century? The use of the imagery of 'Kingdoms' and especially of 'Abbeys' not only provided a carnival reversal of status in regard to a far-away king or a nearby monastery, to whom peasants might owe services and dues; but more important provided a *rule* which the youth had over others and perhaps too a brotherhood existing among themselves; and it gave enormous scope to mockery and derision. *But licence was not rebellious.* It was very much in the service of the

16 Natalie Zemon Davis, 'The reasons of misrule: Youth groups and charivaris in sixteenth-century France', *Past & Present* 50 (1971), 41–75; 74.

village community, clarifying the responsibilities that the youth would have when they were married men and fathers, helping to maintain proper order within marriage, and to sustain the biological continuity of the village. [my emphasis][17]

By the 1970s, against a background of innovative theoretical work in social anthropology and narrative theory, 'play' has become a locus for exploring a dynamic set of exchanges between historicised self-perception and social forms. I am proposing that Natalie Davis's work is in the vanguard of this movement in social history, and that her incorporation of Huizinga alongside Bakhtin and Geertz gives that work a characteristic 'turn', whose influence can be detected in related studies in both history and literature.

Natalie Davis's most achieved, extended use of a methodological approach which resonates with that of Huizinga is also her most famous piece of writing: her 1983 book, *The Return of Martin Guerre*.

The Return of Martin Guerre is the story of an imposter, Arnaud du Tilh, who takes the place of Martin Guerre, a man who has absconded from his family and responsibilities, in the French village of Artigat in the sixteenth century. Du Tilh lives undetected for years with Martin's wife, and lays claim to family properties. Eventually unmasked by family members, the false Martin Guerre is tried and condemned to death. The coup de grace at his trial is the sensational reappearance of the real Martin Guerre to claim his wife and inheritance.

Natalie Davis's carefully historically documented retelling of this tale focuses on the subtle trickery required in order for the substitution of the fraudulent Martin for the real one to work – careful and long-term counterfeiting in everything from family memories to daily behaviour on the part of both Arnaud du Tilh and his 'wife' Bertrande de Rols. Using a wealth of contemporary documentation and archive, she builds up a rich picture of village life in Artigat, against which she sets what detail we have of their lives:

> As I embedded 'imposture' in the cultural practice of sixteenth-century life, so I sought to embed what I called 'the invented marriage' – the relationship that began as a false identity but was sustained by collaboration – in some kind of cultural understanding available to sixteenth century peasants.[18]

17 Davis, 'Reasons of misrule', p. 54.
18 Natalie Zemon Davis, 'On the Lame', *The American Historical Review* 93 (1988), 572–603; 590.

Her methodology (further explicated in an essay published in 1988, in response to a hostile challenge to her treatment of the Martin Guerre story) is that of

> embedding this story in the values and habits of sixteenth-century French village life and law, to use them to help understand central elements in the story and to use the story to comment back on them . . . literary and narrative structure are part of the 'data' upon which I want to do 'vulgar reasoning' to get at a sixteenth-century argument.[19]

At the close of the story-telling section of *The Return of Martin Guerre*, Natalie Davis asks herself a question. How self-consciously did the imposter mould his day-to-day behaviour to that of the man he had supplanted? In court, under cross-examination, according to one of her sources, 'he answered so well . . . he almost seemed to be playing':

> Lawyers, royal officers, and would-be courtiers [comments Natalie Davis] knew all about self-fashioning – to use Stephen Greenblatt's term – about the molding of speech, manners, gesture, and conversation that had helped them to advance, as did any newcomer to high position in the sixteenth century. Where does self-fashioning stop and lying begin?[20]

In her 1988 article, 'On the Lame', Davis elaborates further on why she chooses 'self-fashioning' (a term, she points out, first used by Michel de Montaigne in his essay 'Du dementir')[21] to animate her historical methodology. In doing so, she brings Huizinga's 'play' and the derived notion of 'self-fashioning' sharply together:

> I wanted to extend the concept of forming and fashioning the self to a wider range of situations and social groups – to make it a sixteenth century issue, not just a 'Renaissance' issue. . . . I explore the customs of nicknaming and carnival masking in these regions and the cross into the transgression of taking on a false name in forgery cases, in stories, and finally in the case of Arnaud du Tilh.

---

19 Davis, 'On the Lame', p. 573.
20 Natalie Zemon Davis, *The Return of Martin Guerre* (Harvard: Harvard University Press, 1983), p. 103.
21 'On s'y forme, on s'y façonne . . . car la dissimulation est des plus notables qualitez de ce siècle' (cit. Davis, 'On the Lame', p. 589).

'Imposture' stands not as an isolated form of behavior . . . but as an extreme and disturbing case on a sixteenth-century spectrum of personal change for purposes of play, of advantage, or of 'attracting the benevolence of others'.[22]

***

At the end of 'Reasons of misrule', Natalie Davis comments that the approach she has taken to the forms of play identifiable in peasant communities in early modern France might well be extended beyond 'role-play' to more literal kinds of 'play' – fiction and drama from the period – an invitation to new historicists to join hands, methodologically speaking, with the cultural historians: 'Finally, to literary specialists I may have offered a new source. . . . Is *Hamlet* perhaps a charivari of the young against a grotesque and unseemly remarriage, a charivari where the effigy of the dead spouse returns, the vicious action is replayed?'[23]

I suggested earlier that the core idea that underlies the widely pervasive notion of 'self-fashioning' in social history and literary history today might itself derive from Huizinga. The term 'self-fashioning', in this context, was coined and explicated around 1980 by Stephen Greenblatt, the distinguished literary critic and founder of the critical movement now generally referred to as 'New Historicism'. The term designates a set of critical practices that Greenblatt himself refers to as 'cultural poetics'. Since 1980, I can state with some confidence, New Historicism and cultural poetics have completely transformed the field of cultural textual studies in English-language literary and textual studies.

Here is Greenblatt, in the opening chapter of his groundbreaking 1980 book, *Renaissance Self-Fashioning: From More to Shakespeare*, linking the strategies used by Hans Holbein in his iconic double portrait 'The Ambassadors' with Thomas More's in *Utopia*:

> If there exist highly significant 'blind spots' in *Utopia* . . . they exist like the great, central blind spot [the anamorphic skull] in Holbein's 'Ambassadors': as the object of the artist's profound, playful attention. This playfulness – so easily acknowledged and ignored – deserves special emphasis, for it occupies a central role in both the painting and the book. . . . The distorted skull

---

22 Davis, 'On the Lame', p. 590.
23 Davis, 'Reasons of misrule', p. 75.

in Holbein's painting, for all the grimness of its imagery, is itself an invitation to the viewer to play, while the reader of *Utopia* is invited to enter a carefully demarcated playground that possesses nonetheless a riddling relation to the world outside.[24]

A footnote to this observation makes the connection to Huizinga explicit: '*Utopia*,' writes Greenblatt, 'satisfies virtually all of the conditions of play described by Johan Huizinga, [in] *Homo Ludens*.'

Accordingly, Greenblatt teases out of More's oeuvre a set of strategies he believes More used, to hold at arm's length the constraints and impediments for a man of intellectual integrity, attempting to steer his way through the political thicket of Henry VIII's government and its policies. The idea of linking More's *Utopia* and political 'play' was not itself original to Greenblatt – others with an eye on Huizinga had described his playful irony as '*serio ludere*', adopting a coinage found in fifteenth-century humanist discussion of artful and contrived discourse. But it was Greenblatt who developed Huizinga's insight into an innovative reading practice: if we read *Utopia* as More's way of fashioning himself into a serious commentator on his own political predicament, who employs 'play' to prevent himself becoming entirely enmeshed in the political world he inhabits, then perhaps we have a blueprint for reading other, less directly political, Renaissance authors' way of engaging with the world in which they live.[25]

In the case of Thomas More, Greenblatt suggests, the self-ironising self-fashioning of his early career gave way to a grim objectivity at the end of his life, which sent him ultimately to the block (a shadow perhaps of Huizinga's dismay at the fixed, absolute forms of totalitarianism under which he lived in the 1940s). In the context of *Utopia*, however, Greenblatt's formulation can be heard to derive elegantly from *Homo Ludens*:

> [More's] life seems nothing less than this: the invention of a disturbingly unfamiliar form of consciousness, tense, ironic, witty,

24 Stephen Greenblatt, *Renaissance Self-Fashioning: From More to Shakespeare* (Chicago: Chicago University Press, 1980), p. 24.

25 There is, of course, also a close (and acknowledged) connection between Greenblatt's 'self-fashioning' and social anthropologist Clifford Geertz's methodology for exploring social forms. As, indeed, Natalie Davis pays tribute to the importance of recent work in anthropology by Geertz and Turner. See, for example: 'Social conflict is not something that happens when, out of weakness, indefiniteness, obsolescence, or neglect, cultural forms cease to operate, but rather something which happens when, like burlesqued winks, such forms are pressed by unusual situations or unusual intentions to operate in unusual ways' (Clifford Geertz, *The Interpretation of Cultures* [New York: Basic Books, 1973], p. 28).

poised between engagement and detachment, and above all, fully aware of its own status as an invention. . . . [And] one consequence of life lived as histrionic improvisation is that the category of the real merges with that of the fictive; the historical More is a narrative fiction. To make a part of one's own, to live one's life as a character thrust into a play, constantly renewing oneself extemporaneously and forever aware of one's own unreality – such was More's condition, such, one might say, his project.[26]

***

I have tried to show how Huizinga's *Homo Ludens* provided the inspiration for a loosely associated group of English-language social and literary historians all of whom were looking for a methodology which kept individual and community flexibly in play (and at play) during the creative process. Let me conclude by returning to the general question of Johan Huizinga's importance and enduring reputation as a historian.

In his first and most well-known book, *The Waning of the Middle Ages*,[27] Huizinga argues – in a direct response to Jacob Burckhardt – that the richly realistic, over-decorated art and literature of the late medieval period were not the result of a flowering or flourishing, nor were they an affirmation of cultural confidence. Rather, they were the distraught activities of a community which lived in fear, in a state of constant anticipation of violence, spiritually cowed and politically coerced. In that world, individual experience was so bleak and fraught that the artistically gifted could only concentrate on drowning out the din of dark and dangerous day-to-day life. The pleasure their art gives us is that of a society on the brink of collapse and a culture on the wane: 'Between the absolute denial of all worldly joys and a frantic yearning for wealth and pleasure, between dark hatred and merry conviviality, they lived in extremes.'[28]

Huizinga insists that it is only by paying attention to the intense feelings which saturate his period that it can be properly understood, and lessons drawn from it to inform society's present and future conduct. His strategy is to interrogate the past from a fully emotionally engaged position – as Stephen Greenblatt would put it, '[He] begin[s] with a desire to speak with the dead'. As Huizinga puts it elsewhere:

---

26 Greenblatt, *Renaissance Self-Fashioning*, p. 31.
27 *The Waning of the Middle Ages* (1919; English translation, London: E. Arnold, 1924). The most recent translated edition retitles this as *The Autumn of the Middle Ages*.
28 *The Autumn of the Middle Ages*, translated by R. J. Paton and U. Mammitzsch (Chicago: University of Chicago Press, 1996), p. 24.

There is in our historical consciousness an element of great importance that is best defined by the term historical sensation. One might also call it historical contact. Historical imagination would be too comprehensive and historical vision too definite. . . . This contact with the past, a contact which it is impossible to determine or analyse completely, is like going into another sphere; it is one of the many ways given to man to reach beyond himself, to experience truth. The object of this feeling is not people as individuals nor human life or human thoughts. It is hardly an image which our mind forms or experiences. If it takes on a form at all this remains composite and vague: an *Ahnung* [hunch] of streets, houses, fields as well as sounds and colours or people moving or being moved. There is in this manner of contact with the past the absolute conviction of reality and truth.[29]

It was this passionate concern with the practice of history as the means to 'absolute conviction of reality and truth' that marked out Huizinga's approach to history (he was not, after all, by training a historian) as so distinctive, and brought him to prominence. It also made some of his Dutch colleagues uncomfortable. One of his first biographers, Kurt Köster, called *Waning* – 'the book that was to make Huizinga's name world-famous' Köster says – 'an unusual book', whose importance was not understood for some time after its publication. As another commentator from the late 1940s put it, readers were surprised that 'the rambling colourful tales of the chroniclers had not been consigned to the historical lumber-room, but had been listened to, understood and illuminated by historical perception' – by 'an unusual historical sensorium [sensibility]'.[30]

There was a context for Huizinga's increasing commitment to history as a passionate and emotional pursuit. In 1940 the University of Leiden, where he had been a professor of history for twenty-five years, closed its doors in protest against the dismissal of its Jewish professors by the occupying German forces. In the spring of 1942 Huizinga was arrested and imprisoned, along with other prominent Dutch intellectuals, in the internment camp of Sint Michielgestel at Brabant. Shortly afterwards he was removed from the camp to hospital because

29 Johan Huizinga, 'The task of cultural history' (*Complete Works* VII, 71) cit. W. R. H. Kossmann, 'Postscript', in W. R. H. Koops, E. H. Kossmann and G. van der Plaat (eds), *Johan Huizinga 1872–1972* (The Hague, Martinus Nijhoff, 1973), pp. 223–34; 227.
30 Cit. F. W. N. Hugenholtz, 'The fame of a masterwork', in Koops, Kossmann and Van der Plaat, *Johan Huizinga 1872–1972*, pp. 91–103; 92–3.

of ill-health. For the remainder of the war he lived in exile and under surveillance, with his second wife and small daughter, in the village of De Steeg, near Arnhem on the Rhine. Deprived of his books, and in failing health, Huizinga spent his last years trying to come to terms with the world of which he was now a part. He died just months before Dutch liberation, in February 1945.

In 1943, Huizinga published a short essay entitled 'History changing form', which built upon a briefer piece, 'On a definition of history', written almost fifteen years earlier. 'History changing form' reflects his increasing pessimism about what he sees as the impending dismantling and destruction of European values and culture. Bluntly put, his argument is that you can tell a great deal about an age by looking at the way in which it writes its history – the form and imaginative style in which it is produced. Looking at history-writing in the 1940s, he does not like what he sees.

The main purpose of history, Huizinga wrote then, is to shed light on and make sense of the present. 'History,' he says in the earlier version, 'is the intellectual form in which a civilisation renders account to itself of its past.'[31]

In any period, a community decides what it regards as the values central to it, identifies those features in its past, and imaginatively crafts them into a story which gives sense and meaning to the here and now. In a humane society, says Huizinga, the story of its past can be told with verve and imagination as one which connects us directly with ordinary men and women of earlier times.

In 1943, Huizinga felt that the discipline of history was changing for the worse. It was increasingly concerned with economics, quantitative assessments, mass movements and trends based on numerical analysis. History had got less colourful, less easy to follow, less accessible to the general reader, Huizinga argued, all of which indicated that his own society too had lost its moral bearings:

> Now even in Europe men of science, technologists and statisticians, have driven almost all thought [about humanity] into the corner of purely quantitative valuation. Only the number counts, only the number expresses thought. This shift in the mode of thinking is full of grave dangers for civilisation, and for that civilising product of the mind called history. Once *numbers* reign

31 Huizinga, 'Over een definitie van het begrip geschiedenis' ('On a definition of the term history') *Cultuurhistorische Verkenningen* (Haarlem: H. D. Tjeenk Willink & Zoon, 1929), pp. 158–68: p. 166.

supreme in our society, there will be no stories left to tell, no images for history to evoke.[32]

Earlier I quoted Huizinga's comment on 'fair play' as defining a civilised community's game-playing: 'True civilization will always demand fair play. Fair play is nothing less than good faith expressed in play terms. Hence the cheat or the spoil-sport shatters civilization itself.'

When Huizinga wrote this, National Socialism was on the rise, and the shadow of 'spoil-sports' cast across Europe was a long one. According to Huizinga, absolutist regimes produce fixed, inflexible rules to which communities are forced to adhere, at the same time as they 'spoil' (by suppressing improvisation, individualism and play) the richly generative, life-affirming games of others.

My point here is not that we should dwell on the particular conditions of Huizinga's development of his idea of play as fundamental to understanding the human condition. It is rather in order to point out that there is a strong affinity between Huizinga's fervent plea for a humane narrative history, and the passion with which today historians and critics such as Natalie Zemon Davis and Stephen Greenblatt affirm the possibility of framing a better today by attending scrupulously to the textual and documentary residue of the past. Hence the urgency with which they state their purpose as critics and historians – more than a profession, more of an ethical quest. Here is Stephen Greenblatt:

> I wanted to find in the past real bodies and living voices, and if I knew that I could not find these . . . I could at least seize upon those traces that seemed to be close to actual experience. . . . I wanted to recover in my literary criticism a confident conviction of reality, without giving up the power of literature to sidestep or evade the quotidian and without giving up a minimally sophisticated understanding that any text depends upon the absence of the bodies and voices that it represents. I wanted the touch of the real in the way that in an earlier period people wanted the touch of the transcendent.[33]

And here, finally, is Natalie Davis, narrating her investment in past voices as guiding lights for strong moral values in our present and future:

---

32 Huizinga, 'History changing form', *Journal of the History of Ideas* 4 (1943), 217–223: 223.
33 Stephen Greenblatt, 'The touch of the real', *Representations* 59 (1997), special issue, 'The fate of "Culture": Geertz and beyond', 1997, 14–29; 21–2.

My whole book . . . is an exploration of the problem of truth and doubt: of the difficulty in determining true identity in the sixteenth century and of the difficulty in the historian's quest for truth in the twentieth. 'In historical writing, where does reconstruction stop and invention begin?' is precisely the question I hoped readers would ask and reflect on, the analogy with the uncertain boundary between self-fashioning and lying built into my narrative. . . . I see complexities and ambivalences everywhere; I am willing to settle, until I can get something better, for conjectural knowledge and possible truth; I make ethical judgments as an assay of pros and cons, of daily living and heroic idealism.[34]

The powerful methodological exploration of 'play', sustained and elaborated by new historicists and cultural historians, based on Huizinga's groundbreaking work, continues to stand guard over civilised values, down to the present day.

CODA

On 10 December 2010, a matter of hours before I was due to deliver the Huizinga Lecture at the University of Leiden, I received an email from Stephen Greenblatt, to whom I had sent a copy of my lecture electronically, as I left the United Kingdom. So pertinent was his response to the occasion that I read it out in full at the end of the lecture. It is fitting, I think, to include it again here:

Dear Lisa,

Just a quick follow-up note, now that I have read your essay. You are, not surprisingly, a canny detective. This because you intuited what you could not have known: in 1966–67, when I returned to graduate school at Yale, there was for some reason a shortage of Renaissance teachers. Probably it was just a matter of sabbaticals. Alvin Kernan, who became my doktor vater, taught a Shakespeare course. But in the spring semester Yale had to hire a visiting professor to teach a course, which I took, and that professor was Rosalie Colie. The course, on 17th century poetry, was deeply confusing to me: it was – she was – disorganized, scattered, startlingly erudite, prone to obscure Latin puns, obsessed by a Dutch culture of whose existence I had scarcely been aware, full

---

34 Davis, 'On the Lame', pp. 573, 574.

of winding stairs that seemed to lead to locked doors, brilliant and maddening. At the end of the semester I felt that I had learned nothing and everything; oddly close to her and at the same time completely mystified by her. I still have a few of my books from that course, filled with my notes charged with both fascination and bafflement. In short, the experience of very serious play indeed.

Stephen

Appendix I
'Temptation in the Archives'

Letters from Constantijn Huygens to Mlle Croft

Letters in Worp are 364, 369 (24 Aug 1627), 369a (not transcribed) 'on the same topic' (25 September 1627), 463 (1629), 695 (2 August 1632), 1033 (27 October 1634), 368 (23 August 1627), 823 (15 September 1633).

Letters not transcribed by Worp are transcribed here by the author.

Worp 364 Aan Juffr. Croft [brief summary, no transcription]

Ik neem de gelegenheids waar, u zeer nederig gehoorzaamheid te beloven. 5e Aug.ti, devant Groll, 1627.

KA XLIX-1 f. 375

A Ma[demoiselle] Croft.

Je ne souffriray jamais qu'on me juge aussi indigne de cette belle occasion à vous ~~presenter~~ offrir les ~~asseurances~~ voeux de ~~mon~~ ma tres h[umble] ~~seruice~~ obeissance comme je me le reconnois de ~~l'honneur~~ la confiance dont ~~il plaisa~~ vous voyez que Mons[ieur] le Conte de Hanau me tenait. Aueq vo[tre] permission donques j'essay m'en preualoir pour vous ~~dire~~ asseurer que ce n'est nullement d'aujourdhuij que le bruit ^ nuisant [?] ^ de vous sans merites m'oblige à ~~reueler l'honneur~~ l'ambition de ~~vous~~ pouvoir me signaller M[ademoiselle]

Votre seruiteur et tresobeissant

5 Aug[ust] deuant Groll 1627

Mademoiselle Croft

I would never suffer myself to be judged so unworthy of this fine occasion to offer you assurance of my most humble obedience, in recognition of the confidence which you see Monsieur the Count of Hanau places in me. With your permission, therefore, I will try to profit from it to assure you that it is in no wise today other than the unwonted and unjustified gossip concerning you that makes me presume to declare myself Mademoiselle

Your most obedient servant

Worp 369 Aan Juffr. Croft [partial transcription]

Ik heb beloofd te zullen bewijzen, dat, mogen ook de beide seksen in vele dingen verschillen, beide toch evenzeer door den haartstocht beheerscht worden. Hierbij gaat nu het afschrift van een brief, die dat bewijs levert; de hertog van Bouillon bezit het origineel. Den naam der dame kannen wij niet . . . 24 Aoust 27.

KA XLIX-1 f. 373

Dand^r. Croft

24 Aout. 27 [29 corrected to 27 – later?]

Mad.^{le}

Vous diriez qu'une folle s'est voulu employer exprès à me desengager de la promesse que j'aij ~~promis~~ ^eu la presumption^ de vous faire, lors que l'esperance me fit dire qu'attrapperions un jour de quoy sauuer l'honneur de no[stre] sexe, et promesions à bonnes ensignes que quoy que l'autre soit en possession de mieux p[er]suader, ~~il~~ la passion les gouuerne tous deux egalem[ent]. ~~Sachez mes goie [gelé?], s'il vous plaise, vous en auez~~ ^A cet fois cij les dames m'ont^ de l'obligation de ce que je demeure en la comparaison; car à bien considerer cette enclose, un juge moins neutral les chargeroit d'un ~~bien~~ prejugé bien plus rude. Mais ~~de moy en imaginont a qui je parle~~ moy, le respect de vos vertus ~~relancer m'imposent [?]~~ ^particulierem[ent] me defend^ de penser, à ce qu'il en soit bien difficile de m'empescher de dire ailleurs. C'est donq plustot a vous que reuient l'obligation du sexe, qui faictes ~~irigente~~ [?] croire à la nature, qu'apres vous auoir faicte belle, il soit en elles d'en faire qui vous en rassemblerez. Ce qui ne se trouuant toute fois, aux articles de ma foij, je prie qu'on me dispense de me ~~leerire~~ ^l'aduouer^

que par charité. M[onsieur] le duc de Bouillon garde l'originelle de cette
le[tre], et il semble qu'il ~~lauoit~~ la destinee au plaisir de la Reine, ~~ne~~ si
ne suis-je promis que ~~la~~ ^ma^ copie seruiroit de quelque chose, l'ayant
nettoyeé du mauuois langage Walon qui rendoit la principale moins
intelligible. Les deux petites font encor contre nous. Mais ~~veritablement~~
^de nouueau^ après cette premiere si furieuse, je fay peu de scrupule à
vous donner cet auantage et dans celle qui est sans ~~nom ni superscription~~
^connestre^, il y a du railer [?] beaucoup, et a il esté de scauoir qui est
la dame où elles appartient. mais quoy que nous la con[n]oissons ^de
rais [vrai?]^ et soyons en guerre muete contre ~~ce~~ son parti, j'estime
qu'au moins les dames doibuent estre exemptes de la haine publique
~~mais neanmoins assez offense pour~~ ^y ayant offensé de leur part qui
nous^ oblige a une si cruelle remede que la publications de leurs ~~en~~
amourettes aueq leurs noms. ^et justque vouloir me prendre pittié de
leurs pouures mariz^. Voyez, s'il uous plait, ou me transporte la gloire
de uous entretenir. Ainsi en prend il à ceux qui s'oublient jusque à en
honorer une Vieillarde. Mais tout entrecaidents que vous ~~menvoyez~~ me
^trouuez^ en papier, ne craignez pas la consequence de mes impor-
tunitez de bouche. ~~Au contraire~~ La ^seule^ honte de vous auoir faicte
tort me reculera ~~en faueur~~ de v[ot]re prensence croyant ^tousiours^
que puis qu'auoir ^auant^ eu l'honneur de vous connoistre ^devent
[?]^ j'ay ~~peu~~ esté capable de me dedier a vo[stre] seruice, il sera
possible ci après que sans vous approcher je deuient

Constanter [sign]

KA XLIX-1 f. 372

['A Croft' on reverse]

Croft

Mad.^le

Ma cause n'est pas si mauuaise ~~qu'il ne m'oblige de~~ ^qu'il me faillit^
deuenir faussaire pour la bien defendre, comme il vous a pleu supposer.
~~dans~~ ^par^ ~~la possibilité [?] à les l[ettre]s de monsr. Haddon.~~ C'est
de quoy cette originelle vous a deu faire foy, puisque ma promesse me
defend l'esperance ~~de pouuoir~~ du bien de [illegible crossed-out, ending
~~de bouche~~] ^v[ostre] consideration^. Le respect que je vous doibs
~~m'oblige~~ m'a porté à la faire ma sincerité, que ~~vous tirez [?] indispute~~
^sans subp^r^. vous reuoquez en double^ m'apprendra à l'accomplir.
L'une et l'autre m'obligent a demeurer pour jamais &c

Près de Groll. ~~27~~ 25 7^b. 1627.

Worp 463 Aan Juffr. Croft. [Huygens has later added 1629 at top of page]

Parmi un grand nombre de lettres surprinses de beaucoup d'importance celles ci sont venues à tomber entre mes mains. Pardonnez à la faiblesse de nostre sexe, jusques à ce qu'on aurons attrapé autant de l'autre part, quand un assez imprudent messager de Bruxelles nous fera veoir qu'il y a de la proportion entre les passions des dames de cette cour et la furie de leurs amans. C'est un bonheur que je me souhaitte impatiemment.

KA XLIX-1 between ff. 398–9 barely legible note to Mademoiselle Croft, 1629.

Same drift as the one above. Intercepted letters and indiscretion. Monsieur le duc de Bouillon has the original of the letter of which Huygens sends a copy.

A Mad[ame] Croft. 1629.

Mad[emoiselle]

Vous en auez assez faicte p[our] maprendre aux Cour [vh"], depuis qu'une menteux indigne de vous en portaste la reflexion qu'il vous a plu d'une si courtois [illegible] dans ^ celles ^ mains. J'en ay donq encor revelé cette occasion forceé en esperance que le peu de soubris que ces folies auront le bonheur [?] de vous arracher rendre mon importunité plus supportable. Parmi un grand nombre de le[ttre]s surprinses, de beaucoup d'importance celles-ci sont assures [venues: Worp 463] à tomber dans mes mains. Pardonnez à la faiblesse de n[ostr]e sexe jusques à ce qu'en aurons [attrapé: Worp] autant de l'autre party [part: Worp], quand un aussi imprudent Messager de Bruxelles nous fera veoir qu'il y a de la proportion entre les passions des dames de cette Cour et la prière [furie: Worp] de leurs Amans. C'est un bon heur que je me souhaitte impatiemment, quand est nous serons que pour encor une fois après celle ci auoir subject de vous dire par Courtoisie [?] que je suis

Mad[emoiselle]

Worp 695 [not transcribed]

Evenals gij, voel ik het verlies van den dapperen edelman, nu onlangs bij dit beleg gesneuveld. De graaf van Hanau heeft geweten, welke gevoelens ik jegens u koesterde Le 2e d'Aoust 1632.

[This is same letter as 364.]

Worp 1033. Aan den Hertog van Bouillon [this seems still to refer to the Croft affair]

Je rends tres-humbles graces à V. Ex^e. du tesmoignage qu'il luy a pleu me faire porter de sa bienvueillance par ce sien lacquais. Et ce puisque telle a esté sa volonté absolue et que contre icelle les protestations que j'en ay faictes par ci devant n'ont rien peu valoir. J'ose dire qu'à m'en laisser le choix, je continueroy de vous rendre, Monseigneur, un service non mercenaire, plustot que me veoir serré dans de si estroittes obligations, sachant d'ailleurs trop bien ce que est de mon debvoir à endroict de V. Ex.^e, sans que tant de schandelles m'y esclairent. Mais comme ce n'est pas aux valets de disputer la livrée qu'on leur veult faire porter, je me retiendray d'examiner par quel endroict il me viendroit mieux à poinct que V. Ex.^e m'attachast à soy, et en me soubmettant, comme je doibs, aux arrests de son bon plaisir, luy repeteray tousjours du fonds de mon Coeur, qu'ainsi que j'ay tousjours esté, je demeureray . . . A la Haye, ce 27e d'Octobre 1634.

Worp 368 Aan N. N. (A. B) [not transcribed]

Waarde vriend, waarom draalt gij zoo met aw antwoord? De la Haya. Adi 23 d'Agosto 1627.

Mysterious piece of paper in Leiden Worp volumes [I have corrected from original]

C. H. to Croft, ibidem f. 483

Tout indigné de vous entretenir de loin, qui en ay peu perdre l'opportunité de pres, je vous supplie do ne refuser pourtant a ceste main ingrate, des pacquets de celles, qui ont moins deserui les chastiments des vostres, pour auoir sceu deferer à vos commandements ce qu'elles debruijer [?] moins que moij à l'honneur de voz bienveuil-lances. C'est tout ce que j'ose dire en ceste connecte: jusques à ce que ma soeur [Constantia] de Willem m'aura rendu compte de la priere que je luij ay faicte de vous aller informer du subject de mes impertinences, et de la violence qui, à mon dernier depart de la Haije, m'a empesché de vous aller rememorer ce que je vous prie de veoir tousiours enrolée aux articles de ce que vous croijez aueq moins de reserue au monde, que, partout ce qui se peut jurer de plus sainct, je suis plus que tout ce qui est mortel

[Constanter sign – not in Bachrach's transcription]

This seems to correspond to Worp 823:

Hierbij zend ik u de pakketten. Tot mijn spijt ben ik, vóór mijn vertrek uit den Haag, niet in de gelegenheid geweest, u te bezoeken; mijne zuster [Constantia] de Wilhem zal u daarvan de redden wel meedeelen. Au camp à Dommelen, le 15 Sep. 1633.

Then a fragment – [illegible] 24 Aug. 1627 (f. 573)

. . . proruerons [this word much overtyped and illegible] à bonnes enseignes que quoy que l'autre soit en possession de mieux fendre, la passion les gouuerne tous deux esgalement . . .

[looks like Bachrach's typewriter]

KA XLIX-1 f. 451

A Croft Ce 2 de Aout 1632

Madem[oiselle]

Je me rendroy plus indigne que je ne suis du bon heur de ce grande fortune qui me donner occasion de ~~vous~~ parler à vous, si je n'auraij le juglanere [?!] de m'en preualoir à vous rememorer les asseurances de mon tres humble seruice. Et quand ce pretexte nous manqueroit, n'en ay-je trop plus qu'il ne m'en faut, à vous temoigner ~~le~~ ^ la part que j'ay à vos justes ^ ressentisments de la perte du cher et braue Caval[ier]. qu'apres tant d'autres ce sieijr nous en vain dissimilons . . . [?]

Ma chere damoiselle, ne disputons pas qui de ^ nous ^ deux a le plus deraison de se plaindre et ce desastre. nous auons cette querelle contre tout le monde. Personne raisonnable n'en quitte sa language et son pere sur, mais l'amertume ^ nostre ^ de mon ame m'en preuente ~~de~~ ~~passer outre~~ [replacement text illegible]. fx ainsy les bonsails d'un coeur insensible à moindres acceidisus. Je suis en le faute distance s'en serue, et j'ai affiler à son noble esprit, et je suis à jamais

Ma[demoiselle]

Votre Serviteur Obeiss[ant]

[Possibly refers to Sir Edward Harwood, who was killed at the Siege of Maastricht in June 1632]

Mlle Croft's intercepted letter: Author's transcription and translation

TNA, SP 81/33 fos. 147–50. Calendar entry title: 'Queen of Bohemia's Maid of Honour to a Cousin'. Endorsement fo. 150^v: 'Copie d'vne lettre jnterceptée & deschiffrée en passant entre vne des filles d'honneur de la Royne de Boheme, & vne Damoisselle sa Cousine en Angleterre'. Green refers to this report at p. 245, mistakenly suggesting it is among the State Papers Holland, and also incorrectly suggesting that it must have been written by the Countess of Löwenstein.

Madamoiselle ma treschere Cousine

Pour vous faire resouuenir de vostre promesse, quand vous partistes de Londres en compagnie des autres Dames pour reçeuoir la Royne a Dovres, de me mander nouuelles particulieres de vostre voyage, & de tout ce qui s'est passé digne de notice en allant & reuenant, ie vous ay voulu envoyer vn recueil veritable de tout ce qui a este le plus remarquable en vn tour que le Roy & la Royne, accompagnez de la Princesse d'Orange, ont faict tout fraischement en Northollande: ce que je feray par voye de journal; commençant;

Jeudy le 26.me de Juing quand nous partismes de la Haye vers Harlem en carosse, habillées a nostre ordinaire de voyage, auec chappeaux au lieu de chapperons: ce qui faisoit mesprendre aux bonnes gens qui nous virent passer; croyans la Royne & la Princesse estre yonker William, & Lodouick, & nous autres leurs pages: comme il aduint a vne bonne femme de Harlem, laquelle venant pour voir la Royne, sortit de la Chambre mal contente, disant d'auoir veu trois jeunes hommes a table sans aucune femme en leur compagnie: & le Bourguemaistre dudit lieu visittant la Princesse en sa Chambre la teste nue & le chappeau sur la table ne se vouloit pas couurir le premier, mais insista si souuent sur couurez vous Madame, qu'elle estoit forcée'de prendre son chappeau. Nostre bonheur a voulu que nous nous trouuasmes a Harlem au temps de Kermes ce qui nous presenta la commodité de mander vn grand pacquet de presents a la Haye: lequel y arriua en temps opportun le jour apres, quand le Baron Cromwell faisant vn festin a l'Ambassador d'Angleterre, & toute la bonne Compagnie de la nation a [fo. 147^v] l'Hoff d'Hollande, chacun y trouua sa part: particulierement Monsr St Leger; lequel estant curieux en pourtraicts en reçeut vn mandé de la Royne: dont l'invention estoit vne femme faschée contre son enfant, le batant sy furieusement auec les mains sur les fesses que la sauce en sortit copieusement le tout representé sy naifuement que les jugements des spectateurs n'estoyent pas bastants d'en sçauoir l'autheur: sans que Monsr St Leger (qui a meilleur nez que les autres en semblabels matieres) apperçeut que cestoit de la main de Mabuse./

Le 27.me arriuasmes a Alkmaer, ou nous trouuasmes tous les tailleurs de la ville empeschez a coudre vn lict pour la Princesse. lequel a eu vne courtine [?][1] toute entiere, l'autre du coste & celle du bas bout couppées au milieu a fin de ne cacher point le beau bois du lict: dont on faisoit grand cas. Là nous mangeasmes nostre saoul de grands & beaux posches: & au partir de là la Princesse fut saluée d'vn gras gros baiser a pleine bouche par Monsieur le Bourguemaistre./

En passant par Petten nous mangeasmes tant de m^o^ules, beuuants vinangre au lieu de vin que les coliques prenoyent terriblement la Comtesse de Lewensteyn: mais comme chaque mal a son remede; ainsy le petter a remedie le mal de Petten,: entre lequel lieu & Enchuysen nous passasmes par Medenblick, laquelle ville estant située en l'extremité du pays, yonker William, qui nous trouua là a lentour casuellement, estant reçeu en vne nouuelle charge, sautoit subitement de la carosse de la Royne, & se jettant tout de son long en terre pour monstre son humilité baisa le derriere de Northollande./

Vn grand gros paisant nous seruant ce jour la pour guide des chemins, apprint a la compagnie vne gentillesse nouuelle, de mouscher le nez entre ses doibts, lesquels il essuya quant & quant [fo. 148^r] sur sa barbre: & en recompence de sa courtoisie estant jnvité de manger auec nous, il ne refusa pas le haut bout de table, ny de mettre sa main qu'il auoit nettoyé sur sa barbre le premier dans chaque bon plat; principalement dans vn pasté de benefices que nous pensasmes de reseruer pour nous./

Le 28.me arriuasmes à Enchuysen a douze heures de nuict bien lasses & harassées de la longueur des diques, qui se mesurent en ces quartiers là plus par les miles d'Allemagne que d'Angleterre. Nous y fusmes jncontinent visittées par le Consistoire & jnvitées de faire la cene de lendemain estant Dimanche: mais nous nous excusasmes, estants hors de charité auec les susdites diques, comme aussy auec clochers apres auoir monté celuy de Harlem: qui fut cause que nous eusmes peur d'approcher les Eglises tout ce voyage./

Le Cabinet du Docteur Paludanus[2] est la plus grande singularité

---

1 At p. 349 Royalton-Kisch reads 'courtinance' instead, but there are not enough letters to make up that word.
2 Bernardus Paludanus (1550–1633).

d'Enchuysen: ou entre autres choses dignes d'admiration nous vismes vn certain jnstrument grand, gros, & royde: dont desirants d'estree jnformées, la Comtesse de Lewensteyn plus entendue que nous autres aux secrets de nature, fit au Docteur ceste gentille demande; Mons.ʳ le Docteur ∧ ne vous desplaise ∧ Quel Engin estre la? *questo è* (respond le Docteur, qui nous entretenoit en Italien) *il valente cazzo d'vn Elephante.* Je n'entens pas l'Italien, repliqua la Comtesse. *Hoc est* (dit le Docteur) *membrum genitale Elephantis.* Mais dictes en bon François (repart la Comtesse) ce que cest. Le Docteur se trouuant ainsy pressé, C'est (dit il) vn vit d'Elephant pour vous faire seruice./

Le 29.ᵐᵉ nous touchasmes a Horne: ou le Bourguemaistre, estant vef, desire la Royne de luy donner vne femme [fo. 148ᵛ] d'entre nous autres; & l'election luy estant permise il choisit ladite Comtesse, mais nous entretint aussy toutes de grands complements: comme vous pouuez iuger par celuy qu'il vsa a la Royne le matin de nostre partement, l'abordant ainsy: Madame, vous auez bien besongné pour vous leuez si matin./

Le 30.ᵐᵉ arriuasmes a Edam. Ce n'est pas la plus grande ville d'Hollande; mais nous y rencontrasmes de grands & variables accidents. Le Bourguemaistre nous rencontra hors de la ville, & jnsista fort au Roy, & a la Royne, & la Princesse, de descendre de leur carosse, & faire leur solennelle entrées a pied, ayant a cest effect semé la rue de joncq & fueilles de roses. Là il se presenta a nostre veüe vne jeune fille de 9 ans de meruilleuse grandement haute comme Mons.ʳ Grey, auec lequel elle se mesura: & sy elle continue de croistre comme elle a commencé elle pourra vn jour se mesurer auec l'Elephant de Paludanus. Estants à table au lieu de musique on apporta proche a la Royne vn petit enfant, qui crioit perpetuellement comme vn chat, & en auoit la mine. Vn autre enfant fut mis entre le Roy & la Royne: auquel la bonne femme qui le seruoit donna du pappa de bouche en bouche: ce qu'estant faict a la Hollandese est vne veüe fort agreable & la Princesse en estant particuli-erement delectée, esperant auec le temps d'en auoir vn semblable beut vne santé au Bourguemaistre, qui en estoit le pere: lequel la respondit auec vn grand souspir d'amour, adjoustant ceste parole de consolation; *tis gedaen,*[3] & ainsy luy fit raison./

C'est en ce lieu que nous vismes le pourtraict d'vn homme auec vne barbe sy longue qu'elle ne touchoit pas seulement a la terre, mais aussy estoit retroussée soubs sa ceinture: [fo. 149ʳ] laquelle la Comtesse de Lewensteyn prit pour martes sebellines, dont nous nous en

---

3 Dutch: 'it is done'/'it is over'.

souhaittions vne partie dans nos souliers, a cause que la paué terriblement long & rude en promenant nous faisoit mal aux pieds. Tout ce qui restoit du soupper fut conserué auec grand soing pour en faire collation le matin au Roy deuant son partement & passants par Pourmeren, nous y fusmes menées au *lusthuys* du Bourguemaistre d'Edam: mais nous fusmes forcées de monter quatre eschelles deuant qu'arriuer en haut au lieu de sa plus grande plaisance: lequel estant exposé aux vents de tous costez ne nous sembla pas trop plaisant, outre la peine que nous eusmes a monter & a descendre: & bien heureuse fut elle qui pouuoit bien couurir son Lusthuys de la veüe des spectateurs qui demeuroyent en embassade soubs les eschelles./

Nous disnasmes ce pour là (estant le premier de Juillet) a Moenichedam: ou la Princesse voyant le nombre de petits enfans estre plus grand qu'en autres lieux de Hollande, & en demandant la raison, le Bourguemaistre respondit, que les maisons de la ville estants petites les marys rencontroyent leurs femmes a chaque tour du logis: en outre, que les marys & les femmes, vefs & vefues, se remarient au bout de trois sepmaines: ce que la Comtesse de Lewensteyn approuue pour vne treslouable coustume./

De deux choses furent ils grandement scandalizez par toute la Nothollande comme superfluitez jnnecessaires; premierement la longuer de nos robbes; secondement le nombre de six cheuaux en nos carosses, nous persuadants de raccourcir nos robbes a leur mode, & faisants tant auec leurs voisins d'Amsterdam [fo. 149ᵛ] (desirants de corrigez nostre excez par son contraire) qu'au lieu de six chevaux pour le carosse du Roy & la Royne, on ne leur en donna qu'un pour les mener a leur logis./

Là arrivants le soir du premier de Juillet, nous y trouuasmes l'Ambassadeur Carleton auec Coronel Morgan en attente de nostre venue. Le Baron Crumwell s'y trouua aussy, avec quelques autres officiers Mansfeldiens a la suite du Pagador Dorlbier plus pres a calculer que contez argent. nous y fusmes magnifiquement reçeuz & defrayez (comme par toute la nothollande) par les magistrats du lieu, & entretenus par diuers spectacles: dont les plus fameux furent les deux maisons des Indes-orientales & occidentales. A la premiere trouuasmes vn banquet de noix muscades, cloux de gyrofle, gingenvre, & autres fruicts de l'Orient: ce qui nous fit allez avec grande deuotion vers la deuxiesme, esperants de remplir nos pochettes d'or & d'argent, comme fruicts de l'occident: mais il faut attendre le retour de la premiere flotte. En la balance grande de la maison des Indes orientales la Princesse, se mettant a peser contra la Royne, trouua d'auoir perdu quelques liures de poids depuis quatre ans qu'auons esté au mesme lieu: & en demandant la raison de l'Escoutete: C'est (dit-il) que depuis ce temps là vous avez perdu vostre pucelage: qui est ordinairement vn pesant fardeau aux filles.

Dans le Tuchthuys[4] nous vismes les Chambres au bas pleines des gens de Mansfelt, lesquels sont plus a leur aise que leurs Compagnons en Campagne: & tout en haut le Gouuerneur de la Baya auec ses Jesuites, qui entretenoyent le Roy & la Royne auec force harangues & poesies Latines./

[fo. 150ʳ] Au soir pensants dire a Dieu aux Magistrats en jntention de partir le matin apres au point du joir vers la Haye, le vieux seruiteur de la Royne estant deuenu amoureux de la Princesse, l'embressa & la chatouilla auec tant d'affection, jouant auec les doibts sur les fesses, que la Royne comença a entrer en jalousie, principalement voyant que la Princesse sur la chaude jnstance de son amoureux auoit consenty de demeurer encore vn jour a Amsterdam./

Passans ce jour là & repassans en barque pour voir les bastiments poliz & magnifiques de diuers marchands nous nous sommes trouuez fort souuent enclavez dessous vn pont entre deux escluses, en l'vne desquelles se trouuerent quatre grands batteaux ouuerts chargez d'vne matière fecale, que nous pensasmes estre merde; mais l'Escoutete l'apelloit la richesse de la Campagne: en vne autre nous trouuasmes vn bateau plein d'ordure racle de cuir a demy dressé; dont l'odeur nous fit grand mal a la teste: mais l'Escoutete nous condamnoit pour trop delicats, la louant pour une senteur tresagreable./

La musique a chaque repas apres auoir vn peu choppiné fut composée d'vne espinette, vne viole a costé, & deux voix a table, l'Escoutete & vn des Bourguemaistres fredonnans & beuvants, beauuants & fredonnans au ton & mesure. Cest là que pour acheuer a nous caresser, l'Escoutete presente a la Royne deux gemelles a trois moys d'aage, nommées Becca & Gertrod; ce qui fist penser tout aussytost a la Royne (qui est soigneuse de s'appuyer par bonnes alliances) d'vn double mariage entre lesdites deux gemelles & deux gemeaux nétz a la Haye en son palays depuis son partement, Castor & Pollux enfans de fortune: mais entre les grands il faut du temps pour [fo. 150ᵛ] affaires de sy grande consequence./

Au partir d'Amsterdam nous passasmes la mer de Harlem en vne belle flotte de chaloppes & vn gallion de 20 lastes bien pourueüe

---

4 Dutch *tuchthuis*: house of correction. Royalton-Kisch does not recognise the Dutch and mistakenly transcribes it as 'Zuchthuys' (literally 'house of sighs').

d'artillerie & toutes choses necessaires hormis de viures, n'ayants qu'vne espaule de mouton pour donner a manger a toute la Compagnie: ce qui estoit la prouision de Colonel Morgan, se souuenant de la faim de Breda.

Descendants a luss, my chemin entre Harlem & la Haye, nous y retrouuasmes nos carosses, & vn Ambassadeur du Grand Duc de Moscouie; lequel preuoyant par l'art de divination[5] (qu'est grandement practiquée en ces quartier là) nostre voyage apres avoir presenté a la Princesse ses lettres de creance magnifiquement pliées & cachettées, salua nostre retour par une belle harangue; & ainsy arrivasmes a la Haye le 4me de ce mois vers le soir: ou nous sommes en deliberation d'vn autre voyage a Vtrecht & Amersfort jusques a Deuenter pour voir le fameux cabinet de Mons.r de Smelsing dont je vous rendray conte particulier, demeurant, en attendant de vos nouvelles

Mademoiselle ma Cousine

Author's translation

Copy of an intercepted and deciphered letter exchanged between one of the Queen of Bohemia's ladies in waiting, and her cousin, a young lady in England.

Mademoiselle my most dear Cousin

To remind you of the promise you made when you left London in the company of other Ladies to meet the Queen at Dover, that you would send me special news of your journey, and of everything that happened worth report both going and coming back, I wanted to send you a true account of all the most remarkable things that have happened on a tour that the King and Queen, accompanied by the Princess of Orange, have made very recently to North Holland: which I will do in the form of a journal; beginning thus;

Thursday 26th June we left The Hague towards Haarlem in coaches, dressed in our customary travel outfits, with hats in place of bonnets: which caused misunderstanding among the good people who saw us pass; thinking that the Queen and the Princess were young masters William and Lodovick, and the rest of us their pages: as also happened to a good woman from Haarlem, who coming to see the Queen, left the room dissatisfied, saying that she had seen three young men at table with no woman in their company: and

5 Royalton-Kisch mistakenly reads 'divinaement'.

the Burgomaster of that place visiting the Princess in her Room, she bare-headed with her hat on the table, would not put on his own first, but insisted so repeatedly that she 'cover yourself, Madam', that she was obliged to take up her hat. We were fortunate enough to find ourselves in Haarlem at the time of the Kermesse carnival which gave us the opportunity to send a large package of presents to The Hague: which arrived opportunely the following day, when Baron Cromwell was entertaining the English Ambassador, and all those of rank from that country at the Court of Holland, so that there was something for everyone: especially Monsieur St Leger; who being interested in pictures received one sent by the Queen: whose subject was a woman angry with her child, beating him so furiously with her hands on his buttocks that his 'juice' [sauce] flowed copiously, all represented in so lively a fashion that the judgement of the spectators was not adequate to know the author: if Monsieur St Leger (who has a better nose than others in similar matters) had not recognised that it was by the hand of Mabuse.[6]/

The 27th we arrived at Alkmaar, where we found all the tailors of the town occupied in sewing a bed for the Princess, which had a complete curtain round it, the one on the far side and the one at the end cut in the middle so as not in any way to conceal the fine wood of the bed: which they made much of. There we ate our fill of large and delicious peaches: and as we left there the Burgomaster saluted the Princess with a big fat kiss, full on the mouth./

Passing through Petten we ate so many mussels, drinking vinegar in place of wine, that the Countess of Löwenstein was taken with a terrible colic: but as every illness has its remedy, so farting [petter] cured the Petten illness: between which place and Enkhuisen we went through Medemblik, which town being situated at the extreme end of the country, young master William, who met with us there accidentally, having just undertaken a new commission, jumped suddenly out of the Queen's carriage, and throwing himself headlong on the ground to show his humility, kissed the backside of North Holland./

A big fat peasant who acted that day as our guide, taught the company a new refinement by blowing his nose between his fingers, which he wiped by and by on his beard: and having been invited to eat with us as a reward for his good manners, he did not refuse to sit at the top end of the table, nor to be the first to put the hand he had wiped on

6   Pseudonym of painter Jan Gossaert (1478–1532).

his beard into every fine dish; most especially into a benefice pie [pasté de benefices] which we thought was reserved for ourselves./

The 28th we arrived at Enkhuisen at 12 o'clock at night, very tired and vexed from the length of the dikes, which around there they seem to measure in German miles rather of English ones. We were immediately visited by the Consistory and invited to dine with him the following day which was Sunday: but we made our apologies, the said dykes being out of favour with us, as also were steeples after we had climbed the one in Haarlem: which was responsible for our being afraid to go near Churches for the whole of that excursion./

The Cabinet of Doctor Paludanus is the greatest curiosity in Enkhuisen: where among other things worthy of admiration we saw a certain large, thick and stiff instrument: concerning which the Countess of Löwenstein, who understood more than the rest of us about the secrets of nature, desiring to be informed about it asked the Doctor this amiable question: Monsieur Doctor, if you please, What is this Engine. 'Questo è' (replied the Doctor, who was entertaining us in Italian), 'il valente cazzo d'vn Elephante' [This is the lusty penis of an Elephant]. I do not understand Italian, replied the Countess. 'Hoc est membrum genitale Elephantis' [This is the genital member of an Elephant], said the Doctor. Why, say in good French what it is, replied the Countess. The Doctor, finding himself thus hard-pressed, said, 'This is an Elephant's prick to do you service'./

The 29th we reached Hoorn: where the Burgomaster, who was a widower, asked the Queen to give him a wife from among our number; and being allowed to choose he chose the said Countess, but entertained all of us with extravagant compliments: as you may judge from the one he used when greeting the Queen on the morning of our departure, accosting her thus: 'Madam, you have laboured long and hard to get yourself up this morning'./

The 30th we arrived at Edam. It is not the most sizeable town in Holland; but there we met with sizeable and varied accidents. The Burgomaster met us outside the town, and strongly insisted to the King, the Queen and the Princess that they get down from their carriage, and make their solemn entrance on foot, having to this purpose strewn the road with rushes and rose leaves [petals?]. There he presented before us a marvellously tall young girl 9 years old, as tall as Monsieur Grey, whom she was measured against: and if she continues to grow as she has done so far she will one day be able to be measured against Paludanus's Elephant. When we were at table, instead of music a small child was brought close to the Queen who cried constantly like a cat, and looked like one too. Another child was set between the King and the Queen, whom the good woman who cared for it gave gruel from mouth to mouth, which being done in the Dutch fashion is a most agreeable sight and the Princess was particularly delighted with it, hoping in time to do similarly when drinking a toast to the Burgomaster, who was the father. He replied with a great sigh of love, adding this word of consolation: 'tis gedaen' [that's all over], and so resigned himself./

It was there that we saw the portrait of a man with a beard so long that it not only touched the ground, but was tucked up under his belt: which the Countess of Löwenstein took to be sable fur, a portion of which we could have wished for in our shoes, since walking on the long and rough pavement made our feet hurt. Whatever was left over from supper was preserved with great care to make a morning meal for the King before his departure. Passing through Purmerend, we were taken to the Lusthuys [pleasure house] of the Burgomaster of Edam: but we were obliged to climb four ladders in order to arrive high up in the location of his greatest delight: which being exposed to the winds on all sides did not seem to us particularly delightful, leaving aside the labour we had had in mounting and descending: and one would be most happy who could conceal their Lusthuys from the sight of the spectators who lay in ambush below the ladders./

We dined that day (being the first of July) at Monnickendam: where the Princess seeing the number of small children to be greater than in other places in Holland, and inquiring the reason, the Burgomaster replied, that the houses in the town being small, husbands encountered their wives every time they walked round the house: furthermore, that husbands and wives, widowers and widows, remarried after three weeks: which the Countess of Löwenstein approved as a most admirable custom./

Throughout North Holland people were greatly scandalised by two things as unnecessary extravagances; first the length of our dresses; secondly our using six horses to draw our carriages, persuading us to shorten our dresses in their fashion, and persuading their neighbours in Amsterdam to do the same (desiring to correct our excess by its opposite) so that instead of six horses for the King and Queen's carriage, they were only given one to take them to their lodgings./

Arriving there on the evening of the first of July, we found Ambassador Carleton with Colonel Morgan awaiting our arrival. Baron Cromwell was there too, with some other officers from Mansfeld's regiment, following Paymaster Dolbier in being more prone to calculate than to count money. We were magnificently received there and paid for (as throughout North Holland) by the local magistrates, and entertained with diverse spectacles: of which the most notable were the two houses of the East and West Indies. In the first we found a banquet of nutmegs, cloves, ginger, and other fruits of the East: which encouraged us to go with great zeal to the second, hoping to fill our pockets with gold and silver, as the fruits of the West: but that had to wait for the return of the first fleet. In the great scales of the East Indies house the Princess, being weighed against the Queen, was found to have lost several pounds in weight in the four years since they had been in the same place: and on inquiring the reason why from the Sheriff [l'Escoutete]: 'It is because (he said) during that time you have lost your virginity: which is usually a heavy burden for young women.'

In the House of Correction we saw the lower rooms full of Mansfeld's men, who are more comfortable than their colleagues in the Field: and upstairs the Governor of la Baya with his Jesuits, who entertained the King and Queen with many orations and Latin poems./

In the evening, thinking to say goodbye to the Magistrates, with the intention of leaving at dawn the following morning for The Hague, the old servant of the Queen who had fallen in love with the Princess, kissed her and tickled her with so much affection, playing with his fingers on her buttocks, that the Queen began to be jealous, principally on seeing that the Princess, on the warm insistence of her lover, had agreed to stay one more day in Amsterdam./

Spending that day there and then getting on to a boat again to see the elegant and magnificent houses of various merchants, we found ourselves frequently trapped under a bridge between two sluices, in one of which were four large open boats loaded with dung, which we thought was human excrement; but the Sheriff called it the riches of the Countryside: in another we found a boat full of the scraped filth of half-dressed leather; whose smell gave us a very bad headache: but the Sheriff accused us of being too delicate, and praised it as a very agreeable smell./

The music at each meal after we had drunk quite a lot was made up of a spinet, a viol alongside, and two voices at the table, the Sheriff and one of the Burgomasters, warbling and singing, singing and warbling, in tune and in time. It was there that in order to succeed in making up to us, the Sheriff presented the Queen with twin girls three months old, called Becca and Gertrod; which immediately made the Queen (who is assiduous in supporting herself with good alliances) think of a double marriage between the said twin girls and twin boys born in The Hague in her palace since her departure, Castor and Pollux, children of fortune: but with those of high rank it takes time to settle affairs of such consequence./

On leaving Amsterdam we crossed the Haarlem sea in a fine fleet of launches [chaloppes] and a gallion of 20 lasts, well supplied with artillery and all necessaries except victuals, having only a shoulder of mutton to feed the whole Company, which was provided by Colonel Morgan, remembering the siege of Breda.

Alighting at Luss,[7] midway between Haarlem and The Hague, we found our carriages again, and an Ambassador from the Grand Duke of Muscovy; who having foreseen our voyage by the art of divination (which is widely practised in those parts), after having presented his letters of credit to the Princess, magnificently folded and sealed, saluted our return with a fine oration; and so we arrived at The Hague on the 4th of this month towards evening: where we are discussing another tour to Utrecht and Amersfoort and as far as Deventer to see the famous cabinet of Monsieur [Nicolaas] Schmelzing, of which I will give you a detailed account, remaining, while waiting for your news Mademoiselle my Cousin.

7 Presumably Lisse.

Appendix II
'1688 And All That'

Letter from Christiaan Huygens to Constantijn Huygens

C'a estè une chose bien facheuse pendant vostre longue absence qu'il n'y a pas eu moyen de vous faire tenir des lettres, mais Dieu mercy cela ira mieux dorenavant; du moins les chemins en Angleterre ne seront plus obsedez. Vous pouvez bien vous imaginer avec quelle joye nous avons appris le grand et heureux succes des affaires par de là apres toutes les inquietudes et apprehensions depuis le commencement de cette expedition, soit pour les dangers de la mer soit pour l'evenement incertain de la guerre, car quoyque des votre debarquement les nouvelles aient tousjours estè assez bonnes, l'on ne laissoit pas d'apprehender quelque combat tant que l'armée du Roy demeuroit sur pied, et l'on ne pouvoit pas s'imaginer un renversement si soudain comme celuy qui s'est fait depuis la bien heureuse retraite, que vous ne scaviez pas encore en escrivant vostre derniere a Mad. vostre espouse. Maintenant on attend avec impatience la nouvelle de vostre arrivée a Londres, et de la reception qu'on y aura faite a Mr. le Prince qui sera sans doute une choise admirable a voir. Quelle joye pour la nation et quelle gloire pour luy d'estre venu a bout de cette noble$_{et}$ hardie entreprise. Nous entendrons apres cela comment toutes choses seront establies et reglées, tant par de là qu'icy, qui n'est pas une petite attente. L'on ne scait pas, si vous retournerez ou si vous resterez là/ou vous estes ce qui entre autres n'embarasse pas peu certaine dame que vous conoissez.

(Huygens, *Oeuvres Complètes* 9, 304–5)

Letters from Christiaan Huygens to Lodewijk Huygens

L'on aura dit que par ses dernieres lettres/il ne tesmoigne plus tant cette envie de quiter, que sa Majestè Britannique le traite fort bien, comme ayant dessein de le retenir, avec quoy s'il arrive que sa charge luy vaille bien de l'argent. je ne desespere pas qu'il n'y demeure mais nous n'en scavons pas encore sa resolution finale. . . . Pour moy j'ay bien souvent songè si dans cette occasion je ne pourrois rien obtenir pour amander ma fortune, et j'avois desia quelque dessin de passer la mer pour cela, mais le frere de Z. ayant escrit a sa femme que dans 6 semaines, dont il en est desia passè 3, sa Maj.tè pourroit faire un tour en ce païs, cela me fait differer. C'est dommage que le Prince affectionne si peu les estudes et les sciences, si cela n'estoit point, j'aurois meilleure esperance

(Huygens, Oeuvres Complètes 9, 310–311)

Pour ce qui est du dessein pour l'Angleterre je doute fort s'il en arrivera quelque chose, depuis que je vois que le frere de Z. n'y est pas establide la maniere que j'avois cru qu'il le seroit, et qu'au lieu de cela il semble toujours resolu de quiter le service./S'il fust demeurè, j'aurois pu me resoudre à m'y transplanter aussi, en obtenant quelque benefice ou pension par son moyen ou celuy de mes autres amis. mais puis qu'il n'obtient rien luy mesme, et qu'il ne le sollicite pas seulement, attendant l'occasion de quelque charge vacante en ce païs qui pourroit l'accommoder, je juge bien qu'il n'y auroit rien a faire pour moy, et que je puis epargner la peine et la depense d'un tel voiage. du moins je differe encore'

(Huygens, Oeuvres Complètes 9, 310–11)

Toutefois j'espere que vous voudrez bien me rendre service en cette affaire qui est la premiere dont je vous aye jamais importunè. Je n'ambitionnerois point de charge comme celle la, si ce n'estoit que je vois qu'il m'est impossible de subsister honnestement avec ce peu de bien que j'ay dans ce temps d'exactions, dont on ne voit pas la fin. Au reste cet employ est honorable et assez aisè, qui ne m'obligeroit pas de renoncer a mes autres estudes, et je ne crois pas qu'on doutera si je suis capable de m'en acquiter. Je vous prie donc de ne pas perdre cette bonne occasion de me mettre un peu mieux a mon aise, car en veritè je ne vois rien en ce pais qui soit propre pour moy qu'une des places de ce Conseil, et je regrette de n'avoir pas acceptè l'offre que mon Pere me fit peu devant sa mort de me la procurer en cedant la siene. mais je ne sçavois pas encore que j'e aurois si bien besoin. Le Roy me parla avec beaucoup de bontè lors que j'eus l'honneur de le saluer. Mr. le Comte de Portland me recut aussi fort bien lors que je dinay chez luy avec Monsr. Hambden. Peut estre si vous luy parliez de cette affaire, qu'il ne refuseroit pas de me rendre service. Il y en a qui disent que vous pourriez avoir la place de Petkum comme President du Conseil mais je ne pense pas que vous soiez prest d'accepter ce change'

(Huygens, *Oeuvres Complètes* 9, 335)

Constantijn Huygens junior journal (cit. Huygens, *Oeuvres Complètes* 9, 334, fn. 4): 'Frère Christiaan m'écrivit, qu'il avait été six jours sur mer en allant en Hollande, et me pria de solliciter pour lui du Roi une place dans son conseil, devenue vacante par la mort de Pettekum, ce qui m'embarrassa.'

Christian to Constantijn, 9 September 1689: 'Je vous dis le besoin que j'en aij pour pouvoir subsister honnestement dans ces temps facheux, ou l'on me fait contribuer presque tout mon revenu, et que je ne voiois rien ou je pusse aspirer icy qu'a une charge comme celle la, qu'il y en a qui croient que vous pourriez soliciter pour vous de remplir cette place, mais dans la mesme qualité qu'avoit Mr. Petcum; de quoy/ je doute, quoy que cela vaille la peine d'y penser. Si vous ne jugez pas que ce soit vostre fait, je vous prie de voir s'il y a apparence de faire quelque chose pour moy. Je suis bien fachè de n'estre pas restè un peu plus longtemps a Londres, jusques a ce que cette nouvelle de Petecum fust venüe'

(Huygens, *Oeuvres Complètes* 9, 336–7)

Appendix III
'Never Trust a Pirate'

A note on the clocks involved

Historians of horology have tended to refer to the two clocks used in the extended English trials to Lisbon and Guinea as 'the Dutch clock' and 'the English clock' (in these trials the Dutch clock allegedly performed consistently better). But this is hardly fair. Alexander Bruce's original clock, whether English or Dutch, had been modified according to his requirements in London (by Fromanteel and possibly by Hilderson), while those used on the Hague London trial were once again co-designed by a Dutch-resident Scot and an English-speaking Dutch national, with the technical assistance of Oosterwyck. All the clock-makers concerned were, in any case, of mixed Dutch and English descent. Skilled workers in all their workshops had spent periods of apprenticeship in England and the Netherlands, and, indeed, in France.[1]

Hooke's unpublished Cutlerian lecture responding to Huygens's *Horologium Oscillatorium*: Author's transcription

British Library Sloane MS 1039 fol. 129 Hooke's hand:

Gentlemen

[this para struck through] I am very glad you haue giuen me an opportunity of Presenting the De-signe of Sr John Cutler and of Reading

---

1   See J. H. Leopold, 'Clockmaking in Britain and the Netherlands', *Notes and Records of the Royal Society of London* 43 (1989), 155–65, especially 159–60.

his Lecture <again> in this Place where it was first begun. I think I need not tell you that it was appointed in order to the prosecution of the History of Nature and of art a subject soe copious that tis not to be expected from the single indeauour of <any> one person how able soeuer that there should be any very notable progresse made therein, much lesse from my weak abilityes. But tis from <the> vnited indeauours of the Royall Society <wth> whose <noble> designe <this> is coincident that great product is to be expected, Into whose <Grand> treasury however I shall not (god willing) be wanting to cast in my mite. I haue Lately Receiued from the Inquisitiue Hugenius van Zulichem a book <written by himself> containing a description of seuerall mechanicall & mathematicall Inuentions Intituled

Christiani hugenij Zulichemij test, f. Horologice[m] Oscillatoriu[m] siue de motu pendulorum ad Horologia aplaate demonstrationes geometricae. There are <in it indeed> many things very ingenious and very usefull but there are not wanting also seuerall things that are of a <quite> contrary nature as I shall show you by some few obseruations which I haue made in the Cursory reading of it hauing not yet had time to examine euery particular hereof more strictly.

And in the first Place the Author giues us an account how about 15 years since he first published his Inuention of applying a pendulum to a clock. and thinks <thereby he hath sufficiently secured & warranted> himself to haue been the first inuentor thereof because there was noe body before him that had made publication thereof to the world, and is very unwilling to Allow Gallileo any share in the honour of the Inuention. Whether Galileo or his son did find out a way of applying it to a clock I cannot affirme but sure I am that the greatest excellency of the Inuention is to be ascribed to Galileo who first found out that the vibrations of a pendulum were very neer of equall Duration. Nor Is mersennus or Riccolus to be depriued of their shares in farther examining and promoting the Doctrine of pendulous motions. nor that Franch author who writt anima[te] versions upon Galileos mechaniques who does not only speak of the application of a pendulum to clocks but also enigmatically Describes a way of using it at Sea for the finding out the Longtitude, nor indeed after the knowledge of the equality of pendulous motion was it Difficult to find out a way of applying it to Clocks. D^r. Wren M^r. Rook Mr Bale & others made use of an Invention of D^r. Wrens for numbring the vibrations of a pendulum a good while before Mon^r. Zulichem publisht his and yet did not cry eureka and I my self had an other way of continuing and equalling the vibrations of a pendulum by clock work long before I heard of Mo^r. Zulichems way, nay though equated wth. a Cycloeid yet I have not either cryd eureka or publisht it and yet I think I can produce a sufficient number of Credible witnesses that can testify for it about these 12 years. Soe that the argument that he soe much Relys upon to secure to him the Invention is not of soe great force as to perswaid all the World that he was the first & sole inventor of that first particular of applying a pendulum to a clock.

[over] The next thing wch. he mentions is his invention that all the vibrations of a pend: moved in a cycloeid are of equall Duration. this for ought I know he is the first Inventor of for I never heard of any one that claimed the honour from him of it It is indeed an Invention very extraordinary and truly excellent and had been <honour> enough for him justly to have gloried in the happinesse thereof, and I beleive there is none that would have gone to have deprived him of his Due praise But he should also have Remembred that Golden Rule to doe to others as he would have others doe to him <&> not to have vaine gloriously & most Disingenuously Indeavourd to Depri[ve] others of their Inventions that he might magnify himself and wth. the Jack Daw pride himself in the plumes of others, which how much and often he hath Done in the rest of the book I shall Indeavour to Explaine.

But before I come to these particulars which are indeed noe waye pleasant to me were ther[e] not a necessity & duty incumbent on me to Doe it Give me leave a little to animaduert upon those two Inventions wch. for ought I know may justly be his own. that is the way of applying a pendulum to a clock and the equation of the motion of a pendulum by a cycloeid. For the first I say the Invention is very simple & plaine and therefore soe much the more to be preferred, but yet if thereby the pendulum becomes affected wth. every inequality that the clock work <which it really doth> is subject to and the inequality be not removed by the equation of the cycloeid as certainly & experimentally it is not then be the geometricall subtilty and and demonstration thereof never soe excellent yet it is in it self but a tame invention, and he hath come short by a point if he hath made it dulce & not utile.

First therefore I say his way of applying a clockwork to ye pendulum is imperfect for the pendulum is sensible of every inequality of the motion thereof and though by reason of ye small proportion of the strength of ye water work to the strength of ye pendulum it is not sensible in a single vibration, yet in longer Duration of time it becomes most sensible whence ever the best & most accurate pendulum clocks will sometimes goe faster & sometimes slower sometimes make greater & sometimes lesser vibrations and <having not> produced any invention to make all the vibrations of equall extent he hath not yet produced the invention which can be calld the perfection of timekeeping. For in the 2ᵈ place his invention of equaling the vibrations of a pendulum by a cycloeid will noe ways doe it first because his very first supposition or Demonstration of the nature of the pendulum in a cycloeid does destroy his Imagined theory for if the motion of the pendulum untoucht will make equall vibrations then certainly those vibrations must be unequall if they are sometimes more and sometimes lesse promoted & sometimes more sometimes lesse hindred by the impelling power of the clock work. for though <the vibrations of a> pendulum descending of itself by its own proper gravity will passe either a greater or a lesser arch in the same time the swiftnesse in the greater being to the swiftness in the lesse as the length of the greater to the length of yᵉ lesse but if that droitnesse be altered by an other impelling force then that of gravity then that vibration that hath most impelling force will passe the vibration in shorter time & that wᶜʰ. hath lesse impelling force will passe it more slowly. and is not only in the Descending part of the cycloeid but also in the ascending for though the pendulum left free will ascend either a larger or a shorter arch of the cycloeid in the same time according to the degree of velocity it hath in the perpendicular. yet if that free motion be stopd by a stronger or weaker check of the clock work it shall much sooner or later make its returne and consequently all that equality demonstrated in the theory of the Cycloeid, is by the ile application of the strenght of yᵉ clock work to continue that motion Destroyed soe that we are not any thing further promoted towards equality by this new propriety of the Cycloeid for I judge a pendulum moving in a circle to be a much better measure of time. my reasons are first because as a greater impuls from the clockwork does make a larger & quicker vibration soe on the other side is the larger vibration in its own nature more slow and consequently doth equate and adjust the greater velocity and swiftnesse given by the Impulse of the Clockwork but because this doth not exactly Adjusten and equall the motion of the pendulum it being observed by [opposite, f. 130] Experiment that of a plaine pendulum <clock> will be made to goe slower by hanging more weight to Move yᵉ watch work and to goe some wᵗ faster by taking away some wᵗ of their weight soe that Experiment does seem to hint some middle way of suspending a pendulum between that of a common pendulum & that of a cycloeidi-call pendulum which how it may be done I shall hereafter shew. But in the next place my second Reason why I prefer a common pendulum beyond that of Monʳ. Zulichem is because that moves only upon one center namely the center of suspension <the rod of the Pendulum being

stiff and not at all plyable between the points of suspension and ye Ball> and consequently can have but one kind of Inequality, whereas that of Mon^r Zulichem being <suspended> partly by threads ribands or pliable materiall in order to the bending about the Cycloeid checks and partly also by a stiff Rodd or plate is subject to an other great inequality namely to a bending at the place where the stiff & plyable parts are joynd together. and this is not notionall only but very visible to the eye especially if the check be great that is given it by the watch part. Soe that after all this paines for the adjusting the pendulum after Mon^r. Zulichems way we come short of that Idea of Perfection in the measure of time which his Geometricall Demonstrations would Insinuate were it possible by any of the ways he hath mentiond or Insinuated to make an exact instrument for that end we must therefore seek somew^t Further if we designe to doe any thing accurately in Astronomy not now to mention Geography & the Longtitude because I shall come to that by and by when I come to consider his method of carrying the pendulum clocks by sea. Which is the next thing he proceeds to Discourse of after the Description of his pendulum clock in Generall. but of this I shall Discourse the next Day: And herein he deals very unjustly wth. that noble Person the Earl of Kingkarden who was the first man that attempted to carry the pendulum upon the sea and to Apply it to for the use of navigation and finding the Longtitude describing the story thereof in such a manner as if he himself were the inventor of it whereas tis certaine that he himself drempt of noe such thing like my Lord Kingkardine had made tryale of it, and upon <the Earles> giving him an account of ye successe he was much surprised at the novelty thereof as not thinking it possible as I was heretofore acquainted by the Earl himself when he first brought it into England. nor was that Instrument made ad nostrum exemplum as Mon^r. Zul Hygines would insinuate but of a particular forme of ye Earles owne invention much like this here Described to witt in the forme of a very thick Quadrant loaded at the limb wth. a great weight of Lead & suspended at the right angle by a ball which moved in a Socke which was fastend to the underside of ye Deck of ye Ship. this Instrument being made in holland by ye Earle was brought over wth him into England in order to make tryall of ye Experiment but the verticall being but small and ye weather pretty rough & stormy the watch after some short time stood still soe that nothing could be certainly concluded from it. In february <or march> 1664 as I remember my Lord Kingkarden having gotten another made here in England did togethe[r] wth. my Ld. Brounker S^r. Ro Moray & my self make a further tryall of them wth. some of ye Kings Pleasure boa[ts] but not wth. soe good successe as was expected one of ye watches by the shaking of the boat in the carriage from white hall to greenwich ceasing to goe, & the watches afterwards not keeping exact proportion to one another. they were afterwards sent by S^r. Robert Holmes to Guinny and an account returnd thereof somew^t. like that printed by Hugeinus <made by one of the Captaines> giving indeed a very favourable account of their performan[ce] but concealing all their faileurs & miscarriages whereas another person that was in the same ship gaue a relation very differing. which relation was concealed & the other printed. all this was done before before [sic] Mon^r hygenius had contributed any thing towards this use of them & you may find by his letter wch. was printed in ye p^l. transaction that Major holmes his Relation of ye Pendulums surpassed his Expectation, and that he did not imagine that the watches of this first stracture would succeed soe well. All that I find he added to the Invention was the putting a chaine wth a weight over the ballance wheel which was wound up by the clock work which is indeed not soe good as that made use of by my Lord Kingkarden as I could sufficiently both by Reason and Experience Demonstrate were it necessary but I think it wholly needlesse as being sufficiently satisfyed that neither the one way nor the other will be of any great use at Sea much lesse certainly to find the Longtitude nor will the third that he hath added doe it that having some inconveniences greater then either of the other and noe way removing any of the former. as I shall hereafter shew. however it seems he soe farr prevailed in Holland that the States did Receive his propositions when he Desired of them Patent for those new watches and the recompense set apart for the invention in case of succes[e] and that wth out any difficulty they had granted his Request comanding him to bring one of those watches into their assembly and to Explicate to them his Invention and application thereof to [over] the Longtitude which (in the forementioned epistle printed in the first Philosophicall transactions) he sayd he had done to their Contentment. But not wthstanding we doe not find by this last book of his that he hath yet receivd that reward though it be now some nine years since. nor will he ever <justly> receive it unlesse he find out some other then what he hath yet mentiond.

It was in ye year 1658 <& 59> that I indeavourd to Obteine a Reward from the States for Discovering A practicall and certaine way of Discovering the Longtitude of Places by Sea and Land but upon inquiry concerning such a reward I was answered that there was never any <such> thing, and that it was nothing but a groundlesse fiction the like answer I received Concerning the Imaginary promiceses in Spain

& france. nor could I find any better incouragement here in England where I propounded it in the year 1660. though yet I am sure my way was certaine and very easily practicable and might possibly be the occasion of putting my Lord Kingkarden in nedde [need] of making tryall wth. the pendulum Clocks. But this I mention only by the by and shall hereafter speak more fully thereof when I shall publish that invention and the history thereof.

But to proceed that Experiment that he related to have made wth two pendulum clocks made wth. chaines about the balance wheels is very Strange, and indeed as great an argument against their equall motion when carried in a ship as he could possibly have brought <his words are> for since tis evident by his owne observations and experiments that soe very little a motion as was communicated to the beame by wch. ye Clocks were suspended by one of the Clocks had soe great an influence upon the other clock as to make it inspite of ye unequall lengths of ye pendulums to vibrate together what <change> must not soe great & irregular a motion as that of a ship in foule weather work upon them nor will his new sort of pendulum suspended by threeds triangular wise or the suspension of the clock upon the same center wth. that of ye motion of the Pendulum at all prevaile for the case. for that sort of pendulum being held by these threeds shift in that posture if by the stiffness of the center pinns F & G the clock be any ways out of Perpendicularity the pendulum becomes an inclind pendulum and consequently moves toe much ye slower and consequently receives a variation from the motion wch. is the thing which he indeavours to obviese [?] but hath noe ways found a means to doe.

And indeed if one well considers the manner of suspension it seemes very rationale to suppose this manner of suspension much worse then my Lord Kingkardines for in this of Huginius the motion of ye vibration of the machine being upon the same center wth. ye vibration of ye pendulum the motion of the one is the more likely to confound the motion of ye other. then when the motion of the machine is upon a point a good way removed from the center of ye vibration of ye pendulum either above or below. And thus much may suffice for the things mentiond in the first part of his book wch. is a Description of the Instruments themselves.

[circa 1676 from internal evidence]

Appendix IV
'The Reputation of Sir Constantijn Huygens'

Madame de Stafford, à qui j'ay rendu vostre lettre, après quelques delays, m'a dit enfin que le Sieur Lainier et autres de la Musique du Roy jugent que l'accord de violes, que j'avoy trouvé, est très-excellent et rare, et vault bien le prix de trente livres *sterling*, duquel ils n'avoient rien peu faire rabattre; dont je fu bien estonné. ayant espéré de l'avoir à meilleur marché par son adresse, mais je croy plustost que l'enqueste trop curieuse de plusieurs qu'elle y a employée n'a fait que le renchérir. Quoy qu'il en soit, après avoir marchandé extrèmement moy-mesme, je l'ay acheté à la fin (de peur d'estre prévenu par un autre) pour vingt-et-sept livres et demye *sterling*, pardessus un chapeau gris d'Hollande, que vous envoyerez, s'il vous plaist, et que/les instruments vous aggréent bien, quand quelque messager ou autre s'en viendra icy. J'ay fait embarquer lesdits six violes (enfermez et bien accomodez dans une casse ou bahu) en un bateau de Middlebourg, dont le maistre, qui s'appelle Laurens Soeteling, m'a promis d'en avoir grand soing, et de l'envoyer seurement par la barque ordinaire de ladite ville tout droit à La Haye. J'ay payé huict shillings *sterling* pour touts les fraiz de l'embarquement et transport jusques en Zelande, et attendray icy le remboursement e l'argent à vostre commodité, n'en ayant pas à faire en Hollande, d'où il faut que j'en tire moy-mesme par lettres de change

(University Library Leiden, Worp, nr. 2035, Cod. Hug. 37, transcribed by Rasch, pp. 299–300)

Ick sendt UE de baseledt van amber voor Mevrou Killegrew. Ick ben blij, datter iet is dat sij van mijn begeert. Dat en al dat ick heb in de waerelt is om haer te dienen. Sij salt te veel eer aan mijn doen, dat sij t dragen sal, warme sij mijn grootelijckx sal verobligeeren. Segt haer, dat het compt van eene, die haer diners meer is also oit imant geweest is, niettegenstaende alle haer liefhebbers. Mijn is leet, dat sij vandaer vertrocken is, omdat UE daer vermaeck hebt in huijs kennis te hebben. Doet toch mijn dinstighe gebidenis aen haer goede graci. Segt, dat sij wel mach geloven, dat ick haer liefheb, want ick gun haer van herten deselfde vreucht, het haer toch. Ick bidde, vergeet niet het rinckxken, dat sij mijn beloft heeft. Sij is soo leelijck geworden, dat het ongeloflijck is. Hij siet er al vrij wat betrout of berout uut

(Worp, nr. 242)

Je pense m'acquitter d'une vielle debte, en vous offrant ces tailles douces. Au moins ma maison me semond d'un peu de mention que je vous ay faict autrefois de ce batiment. Soit obligation anciene ou nouvelle importunité, voyci le morceau de brique que j'ay eslevé à la Haye, en un lieu, que j'ose bien nommer des plus illustres du village. Quand je l'entamoy, la main de l'Eternel ne s'estoit encor appesantie sur moy. Je vivoy doublement, dans la saincte compagnie de *Lei ch'è salita A tanta pace, e mi'ha lasciato in guerra*, et d''où je ne puis *seno haver l'alma trista, Humidi gl'occhi sempre, e'l viso chino*. C'est ce qui me porta à ceste égalité reguliere de part et d'autre, que vous trouverez en ces departemens, que vous sçavez avoir tant pleu aux anciens, et que les bons Italiens d'aujourd'huy recerchent encor aveq tant de soin, distribuant les quartiers des deux chefs de ma famille en deux sales, deux chambres, deux garderobes, deux cabinets et autant de galeries. Le tout separé par une sale d'entrée ou vestibule, et couplé sur le derriere par la communication d'un passage privé. Aujourd'huy ce qui avoit esté destiné pour la mere, sert aux enfants et à ceux quiles gouvernent; ma portion est du costé du jardin, que je decouvre à gauche; à droicte tout ce qui sort et entre par la bassecour; et sur le devant une excellente plaine, ceinte de bastimens, que grands, que mediocres. close de deux rangs de tilieux au croissant de leur aàge, et rebordée d'un pavé de ruë de 36 pieds, dont le costé que flanquent les saillies de mes galeries s'estend en ligne droicte à quelques mil pas. Je vous prie de jetter l'oeil sur le reste, et de m'en dire franchement vostre advis. Si vous ne me donnez que l'approbation que, possible, j'auray meritée en quelqu'endroict, j'estimeray que vous me cachez la censure qui me pourroit servir d'instruction et à d'autres d'advertisement. Mon dessein estoit d'adjouster à ces imprimez – dont je garde les planches à moy seul – une sorte de dissertation latine à mes enfants, par où, apres moy, ils demeurassent informer des raisons et justifications de mon faict, et me fusse-je lairré [laissé] entrainer, à ceste occasion, en des considerations non inutiles sur le subject de l'architecture anciene et moderne, mais les divertissemens de mes charges occupent jusques à present la pluspart du loisir que cela requerroit. Je verray, si ces moiz de campagne m'y fourniront ce que la garnison me refuse, et en ce cas retoureray à vous faire part de mes resversies [reveries?], sachant combien vous avez deferé à ceste estude par le passé et aveq combien d'applaudissement. Son Alt.sse s'est rejouïe de vous sçavoir relevé d'une forte maladie, depuis laquelle apprenant que vous avez encor ramené la main au pinceau, elle m'a commandé de sçavoir, si vous auriez [seriez?] aggreable de luy embellir une cheminée, dont les mesures vous seroyent envoyés, de quelque tableau, dont l'invention fust toute vostre, comme la façon, qu'on ne desireroit de trois ou quatre figures pour le plus, et que la beauté des femmes y fust elaborée *con amore, studio e diligenza*. J'attendray, s'il vous plaist, quelle inclination vous y avez et, pour toute la miene vous asseureray, qu'elle bond de passion à vous faire veoir aux occasions de vostre service, que je suis . . . 2 July 1639

(Worp, nr. 2149)

Du reste Monsr, ce gros pacquet vous dira comme je reçois sans raillerie le compliment que me font mes amis des effectz de leur amitié et bons offices. Ce sont les/figures de ma mauuaise Architecture que j'auoy pieça [déjà?] promises à Madame Killigrew (dite Stafford aujourdhuy) et me trouuoy bien en prinse par quelle voye les faire passer deuant Duynkercke où je seroy bien marry qu'on dist que jeusse l'ombre seulement de quelque chose à moy. Maintenant que voz gens vous traineront plus d'un coffre, je vous supplie tres humblement que dans le moins important de tous il se puisse trouuer un coing pour ce roulleau et qu'un lacquay ayt la charge de l'addresser à vostre arrivée. J'y adjouste un second exemplaire pour vos peines, sachant bien qu'en ces occasions de voyages ona besoing de beaucoup de papier a seruir d'enueloppe au baggage

Huygens to William Boswell

(28 June 1639, Den Haag, Kon. Bibl., Hs. KA XLIX, f. 903, Worp, nr. 2145, transcribed by Bachrach, pp. 354–5)

Il s'est trouvé que le luth est absolument le plus beau et meilleur luth de Boulogne qui soit en Engletterre, de la grandeur ainsi que le désirez, plustost plus grand que petit; il est à neuf cottes et de Laux Maller. Il est barré et enmanché par Maistre Nicolles que ne [nous?] tenons icy pour le plux ecellent qui soit icy pour le barré. Et pour les reste aussi, c'est un luth propre à chanter aussi qu'à jouer des piesces. Ayant monstré vostre lettre à ce gentilhomme, à ma prierre il [l']a voulu laisser aller. Le pris est dessus de telles conditions que ne serez forcé à rien que cet qu'il vous plaira, qu'est que le gentilhomme et moy nous nous obligons par escrit à Monsieur Rivait, que, cy n'agreez le luth, le renvoiyant, nous rendrons la somme, que sera trente livre esterlin. Je ne vouldrois pour toutes les choses du monde faire aucune action pour vostre service qui ne fust cincère et naitte et sans aucune falcification. À mon jugement le luth est le plus excellent que j'aye jamais ouy de sa grandeur.

Gaultier to Huygens, *c.* 30 April 1645

(University Library Leiden, Cod. Hug 37, Worp, nr. 3953, transcribed and replaced in the right 'Worp' order as nr. 3940A by Rasch, pp. 719–20)

Je vous diray doncq, Monseignieur, touchant le luth que désirez avoir de moy: Madam Staford m'en a parlé sans rien conclure, estant malaise. Si vous n'entendez mes raisons: ledit luth a esté choisi dans une quantité d'autre venant de Bolonnie et le seul de Laux Maller mort cent cinquant ans passes, et achetté par un nommé Jehan Ballard, jouer de luth de Sa Majesté, et luy a coutté soixante pistolles, le corps et la table seullement, depuis l'ayant fait acommoder et apporté en Angletterre. Durant la vie dudit Jehan Ballard. Jamais le Roy n'a sceu avoir ledit luth pour aucun argent ou menace que se fut, l'homme venant à mourir, et le luth et demeuré entre les mains de quelques pauvres parans qui aprais plusieurs debats et marchez a-t-on donné cent livre esterlin. Et après le Roy me l'a donné qui est la seule chose que j'ay de reste après trent anné de service. Et l'excellence d'un bon luth augmente ou diminue le jeu d'aucune personne. Je vous laisse don, Monseignieur, le juge de cette affaire. Il n'y aura jamais personne que vous qui l'aye pour quelque grand somme que se soit, et pour traiter avec vous comme avec celuy que j'onore au dernier point, si l'avez agrable, je vous envoiray le luth et in jourez et le montrerez et comparrez ainsy qu'il vous plaira est peult-estre que l'humeur vous passera et serez raçasié, et ayant joué, pourveu que me le renvoyez sein et sauf, je seray content. Et si le desireis avoir, le pris sera ce qui l'a cousté au Roy

(University Library Leiden, Cod. Hug. 37, Worp, nr. 5223, transcribed and renumbered as Worp 4950A by Rasch, pp. 944–5)

Appendix V
'Dear Song'

Letters from Constantijn Huygens to Dorothea van Dorp

J. A. Worp, *De Briefwisseling van Constantijn Huygens (1608–1687)* ('s-Gravenhage 1911–1917), now checked against online edition which reproduces originals http://resources.huygens.knaw.nl/ briefwisselingconstantijnhuygens.

Worp 56

A mon retour de Bagshot, où nous avons employé toute la septmaine passée, je me suis estonné de ne trouver de vos letters au logis. Pour ce qui est des miennes, je m'asseure qu'en aurez receues deux presques à la fois, dont la nonchalance du porteur de la première a esté cause, comme les dates vous pourront faire croire. La présente va de compagnie avec deux pastez de vénaison, desquels Monsieur mon hoste vous envoye l'une, et l'autre au Greffier Aerssens, ayant change de resolution qu'il avoit prise d'en envoyer deux à Son Excellence pour des considerations qu'entre autres siens amis je luy ay mises en cervelle. Ce sont les quartiers d'un cerf qui à donné de la peine au Roy depuis les dix heures du matin jusqu'aux onze du soir, quand finalement, ayant desjà deux blessures au corps (l'une de la main du Roy), Monsieur le Prince luy bailla le coup mortel avec son arbaleste justement dans le Coeur, ce grand animal nageant plus de trois quarts d'heure dans un grand/vivier, où il se pensa sauver. Dont pourrez conclure s'il vault la peine d'estre mangé en reverence et attention. Je me souviens avoir promis par jeu à Mademoiselle van Dorp de luy faire manger de lavenaizon d'Angleterre; je vous prie qu'à cette occasion elle en puisse avoir sa part

Worp 80. Aan Dorothea van Dorp

Songetgen. Je me trouve esloigné de vous de beaucoup de journées. Cependant je vous asseure du dedans de moy, qui vous demeure perpetuellement affectioné apres ceux que Dieu et nature me font honorer autant qu'aimer, je trouve mon grand contentement au resouvenir de vostre amitié, laquelle je voudroye vous pouvoir exprimer combien j'estime. L'occasion ne veut pas que j'en jouïsse en presence; au lieu de cela je desire que les miens en puissent tirer contentement et proufit. Ce sont mes bonnes soeurs que je vous recommande et supplie de leur vouloir servir de salutaire exemple, continuans tousjours parensemble cette honeste amitié que je me vante d'avoir gardé quelques années avec vous. Je souhaitte qu'elles puissent tirer de vous ce que j'eusse desiré qu'eussiez proufité de ma conversation. Prestez leur la main au chemin de la crainte de Dieu, qui est la source de toute vertu, et je m'asseure que vous les trouverez sorties de l'apprentissage de deux honestes et soigneux parents qui n'y ont rien planté que bonnes herbes, qui doibvent s'avancer quelque jour en des fruits saints et salutaires. Je ne touche point au soing que devez avoir de vous mesme, car vous mesme vous le sçavez; en un mot, faites moy l'honneur de vous resouvenir quelquefois de ces exhortations à gravité et modestie dont je vous ay battu les oreilles si souvent. Si les plus avisez ne s'y conforment, je veu qu'à tousjours mais ma parole soit hors de credit chez vous. Or, *Thehen*, Dieu sçait que je soigne de bon coeur à l'avancement de vostre bonne reputation, pour vous aider à la rendre impenetrable à toute sorte de calomnie. Je suis vostre sincere ami, donc je vous parle rondement; si cela vous deplait, j'en dois estre adverti en temps. Voici des pieces mal cousuës que je verse en toute haste environ minuit, mais le contentement de parler avec vous m'oste tout autre souvenir. *Kint*, ne vous alienez jamais de moy, et que pour si peu de mois je ne puisse trouver du changement en vostre coeur; c'est cettuy la seul que je m'approprie; resolvez du reste comme maistresse du logis, je n'y pretens rien. Mais encor, si peut estre en mon absence l'envie vous prend de vous engager à quelque autre – vous, je supplie, choisissez le un peu selon mon humeur, et vous reglez au petit contentement de celuy qui fait estat de vous continuer une immortelle amitié, mesme aprez le jour qui vous aura rendu proprement propre à un mari, car, *Thehe*, ce me sera un des grands plaisirs de vous pouvoir trouver en vostre mesnage, si notament le chef en soit tel et qualifié comme je vous le souhaitte. Je remets tout à vostre discretion et apprens mon scel desasteure à tout ce qui resoudrez. Adieu Kint, j'attendray de vos lettres à Venise. Si vous desirez nouvelles de nostre voyage, enquestez en vous chez nous ou à la Plate, de buermeyt [eene der drie dochters van François van Aerssen. De families Huygens en van Aerssen woonden dicht bij elkander in het Voorhout]. Den Trello, de Van Santen, den Dimmer et toute la cabale soit saluée s'il vous plait tres affectionnement en mon nom. Devant touts Mad[ame] d'Eussem, etc. Mandez moy si avez receu le pourtrait. Adieu, adieu. En haste de Stutgard, au païs de Wirtembergh, ce 18e de May 1620.

Worp 84. Aan Dorothea van Dorp

Lieve Songetgen, Je derobe ce moment de temps de l'importunité des mes affaires, pour me condouloir de la maladie qu'on me faict sçavoir vous avoir surprise. Quelle en esté ou la qualité ou la cause, je ne le sçay point; bien puis je juger que c'a esté quelque chose d'extraordinaire qui vous a empechée de me continuer la faveur accoustumée de vos lettres. J'espere que l'espoir que m'a donné mon frere de vostre guerison n'aura esté en vain, et que hormais vous estes hors de peine. Parmi les triomphes et magnificences qui nous ont accompagnez depuis qu'avons mis le pied en ce païs delicieux, je n'ay jamais manqué de raffraichir la memoire de vostre amitié et conversation, qui me valent plus, sans comparaison, que toutes ces splendeurs du monde. De ce qu'avez prins la peine d'aller entretenir mon bon pere en son infirmité, je vous en ay de l'obligation comme d'un debvoir presté à ma personne. Ne permettez jamais que cette amitié entre vous et les nostres defaille, et vous ne vous en plaindrez point. Remercie Mad[ame] Trello de sa jolie lettre qu'elle me faict l'honneur de m'escrire; je l'ay prise pour d'autant plus solides asseurances de son affection envers moy, qu'une parole vault mieux que dix pensées. Pour m'excuser de ce que je manque à luy respondre, montrez luy seulement ce mot, qui le fera bien juger comme le loisir m'a esté cher et escart (?) [sic]. Adieu *Songetgen*, ne doubtez point que je ne soye tousjours vostre ami indubitable. Mais de grace escrivez moy à toutes occasions. Si la prochaine fois il me reste quelque peu de temps d'avantage, je vous communiqueray certains miens advis qui me sont venus en cervelle par chemin, comme en cheminant à cheval on a loisir de penser et repenser dix mille choses sans destourbier. Tenez toujours bonne amitié avec Edmond, mais temperez vos actions avec cette discretion qui vous est naturelle. Aprenez de moy que, si vous vous jettez vous mesme, personne ne vous relevera. Je veux du bien à S[eigneur] Thomas, mais à vous aussi et à touts deux ensemble; c'est pourquoy je souhaitte quelque jour de venir à bout de quelque bon dessein, mais en reputation et honneur. Un autrefois plus à plein de ceci. Mais baisemains à M[adame] d'Eussum, Santenskint, Trello, Dimmer, Claesje, Kilgrew, Mess[ieurs] vos freres, Edmond, Connervay et tout le Voorhout. Adieu *Kint*. De Venise, en courant, 18e Juin 1620.

Worp 177. Aan Dorothea van Dorp

Songetgien, Vostre voyage de Kenenburgh m'aggrée pour la mesme raison qui vous l'a rendu moins agreeable; il est bon d'avoir à faire parfois à des gens d'opinion contraire à la vostre pour se roidir à la defense de chascun la sienne et, par voye de dispute, se descouvrir soy mesme à soy et sçavoir combien c'est qu'on sçait. Puis on aiguise sa trenche à la frotter à l'acier de l'obstination des ignorans; c'est ce qui a donné occasion aux premiers disputes d'escole, ou elles s'appellent les espluschements de la verité. Mais aussi apres l'avoir acquise, il reste le grand point de la pratique qui s'enseigne hors des escoles, ou au moins exercée avec moins d'aigreur. Cette pratique, comme en touts les chefs de nostre foy, ainsi notamment en ces dernieres controverses, doibt estre la visée et le but de l'exercice, afin que l'ame, s'estant eslancée de tout son pouvoir jusques au plus haut degré de l'election absoluë de Dieu, se regarde par apres au dedans et, asseurée de ce qui est de la racine de l'arbre, en vienne par apres aux fruits, esquelz la dependance du haut avec le bas luy doibt fournir tout le subjet de sa consolation et l'asseurance de son salut.

Si apres vostre retour à la Haye mes soeurs vous ont esloigné les apparences du mien, elles vous ont fidelement communiqué mes derniers adviz, que je ne sçauroy desdire pour encores. Le temps de neuf moiz à la verité est tres-long pour une ambassade extraordinaire, mais encor nous consolerions nous en la misere commune de vostre sexe, si au bout de ce terme peussions nous descharger le ventre d'un fardeau si importun. Je n'y voy nulle apparence et en mon particulier toutefois m'appaise des raisons que vous ay souvent alleguées. Cependant de loing je considere comme spectateur l'effroyable estat de ma patrie et, ne fut que j'esperasse en la providence de l'Eternel pour le regard de la manutention de sa propre cause, la representation de noz mauvaisetez me feroit desesperer de sa merci. Je le prie de coeur, qu'il vous la continuë en vostre particulier, comme je suis d'affection interne vostre ami tres-ami

Den Song.

Mes baisemains à Mad. Vostre hostesse avec tous les siens, *'t schoone kint* devant tous. Je m'attends à la promesse que me faictes de m'aviser des amours de mon bon frere; il me contente infiniment d'entendre l'heureux estat auquel à present se rencontrent tous les troiz vostres. Londres, ce 11e de mon mois (Sept.) 1622.

Worp 242

Ick sendt UE de baseledt van amber voor Mevrou Killegrew. Ick ben blij, datter iet is dat sij van mijn begeert. Dat en al dat ick heb in de waerelt is om haer te dienen. Sij salt te veel eer aan mijn doen, dat sij t dragen sal, warme sij mijn grootelijckx sal verobligeeren. Segt haer, dat het compt van eene, die haer diners meer is also oit imant geweest is, niettegenstaende alle haer liefhebbers. Mijn is leet, dat sij vandaer vertrocken is, omdat UE daer vermaeck hebt in huijs kennis te hebben. Doet toch mijn dinstighe gebidenis aen haer goede graci. Segt, dat sij wel mach geloven, dat ick haer liefheb, want ick gun haer van herten deselfde vreucht, het haer toch. Ick bidde, vergeet niet het rinckxken, dat sij mijn beloft heeft. Sij is soo leelijck geworden, dat het ongeloflijck is. Hij siet er al vrij wat betrout of berout uut

Worp 310. Aan Dorothea van Dorp.

Song. Mons[ieur] vostre frere m'envoya hier au soir vostre lettre, sur laquelle cette ci va de response, pour vous dire que là où luy ou quelqu'un des vostres pourra avoir besoin de mes advis ou adresses, je m'y employeray de pleine affection, de sorte qu'on ne desirera jamais rien en moy que le pouvoir de vous obliger tous, la volonté m'en demeurant tres parfaicte. Pour les differents où ce voisinage est tombé passé quelque temps, je n'y pretends part ni portion, et croy qu'entamé par les femmes il pourra estre vuidé de mesme, mais, comme j'ay dit, si vous vous en rapportez `a l'entremise de ces gens icy, il n'e ira que de mal en pis; à faute d'instruction sur le principal ilz sont capables de s'esgarer et s'en prendre où ilz en ont le moins de subject. Je n'ay pas esté present à cette conference que Mad[ame] van Dorp a eüe avec ma mere et dont elle vous aura donné advis sans doubte, puisque peu sagement on la faict esclatter devant ceux qui en ont bien peu à faire. Mais si elle persevere à me charger de blasme, comme j'apprens que desja de travers elle s'est meslée d'y toucher, je me verray enfin forcé à faire ouverture de mes livres, et l'asseure bien qu'elle y lira sa confusion et ma sincere affection pour le service d'elle et des siens, n'y ayant que l'ingratitude qui la puisse disputer. Mais le desir de paix et concorde qui me gouverne dessus tout me faict esperer et souhaitter que le proces sera vuidé devant que j'aye besoin de cetter production, et que, s'il plaist à Dieu, l'estrif se terminera en risée un jour; ce que je ne di pas certes par defiances de nostre cause, car j'estime qu'elle se defend soy mesme et que pour la combattre vous aurez besoing de bons coups d'escrime, mais, encor un coup, par pure envie d'union et d'amitié à laquelle je porteray tousjours autant que pourrez desirer du

Song.

De la Haye, ce 11e d'Avril 1626.
Mes recommandations à tout le monde.

Worp 311. Aan Dorothea van Dorp.

Song, Apres que mes occupations m'ont faict fausser trois jours de suitte le debvoir de vous respondre et à quantité d'autres amiz qui se plaignent de mesme stile que vous, encor aujourdhuy me bornent elles mon loisir de si près que je ne sçauroy que vous dire en tres grande haste qu'à mon advis Mons[ieur] vostre frere fera bien de se presenter devant le Prince à cet heure qu'il doibt aller songer à disposer d'un si beau commandement. L'admiral m'asseure qu'il aura sa voix et que ce seroit luy faire tort de ne le luy donner point. Mais puisque la resolution en est cachée au coeur de mon Maistre, où peut estre elle n'est encore conceuë, c'est chose doubteuse d'en juger.

Le S[eigneur] Calvart nous avoit desjà donné l'alarme de vostre maladie, qui m'estonna du commencement, mais apprenant qu'un peu plus d'apprehension qu'il ne faloit pour si peu de mal vous avait fair fare la mourante, quand grace à Dieu il n'en estoit guere temps encore, j'ay faict du complaisant à me rire de ce que d'autres me disoyent avoir esté ridicule à veoir, lorsque vous prinstes congé des parens et vous imaginastes d'avoir la mort au bout des ongles. A cet heure à mon advis vous la faictes trop longue là, et des mescontentemens que voz amis ont conceu contre vous ne se debattent pas ici à vostre advantage, comme je me promets que vous vous en sçauriez defendre en presence. Je voy naistre des inconveniens de ce qui tout le monde ne sçait pas le fonds des affaires et d'autres ne le veulent pas sçavoir. De moy j'ay tousjours des trouppes de reserve, qui au pis aller me garantiront de toutte calomnie, mais comme je suis marri de veoir du desordre parmi des amiz, aussi voudroy-je que prinsiez la peine de les venir developper, au lieu d'autres, qui par faute d'instruction peuvent rendre vostre cause pire qu'elle est. Le reste de vostre belle lettre et celle que vous laissates icy sont l'infirmité mesmes et ne meritent point de response, si n'est que je suis tousjours le mesme de coeur et d'intention que j'ay esté tousjours et le seray pour tous changemens qui puissent arriver au train de ma vie, sçavoir

den Song.

Recommandations partout, s'il vous plaist.

342. Aan Dorothea van Dorp.

Vous avez tant eu la teste rompue de mes intentions, qu'il m'a semblé que la communication de cetter derniere ne se pouvoit faire en aucune part à moins d'offense. Je veux dire quie vous portez comme une cicatrice l'importunité de mon entretien et que par ainsi vous avez moins de sensibilité aux coups nouveaux. J'enfantay cette conception pierreuse aujourdhuy dans mon lict, pour vous dire que les *Bruygoms* comme moy se donnent assez de loisir à porter ailleurs la pensée qu'au pucelage de la maistresse. C'est bien vous qui me cognoissez des mieux, mais apprenez qu'en ces entrefaittes, où volontiers la pluspart du monde s'oublie, je m'esvertue à ne rien faire qui oblige ma ressouvenance à me faire rougir ci apres. C'est en partie pour vous conserver entier l'honneur qui vous demeure de m'avoir nourri et eslevé sagement. J'attens qu'à tout heure on m'apporte la nouvelle du choix que Mess[ieurs] de Zelande auront voulu faire de la personne de Mons[ieur] vostre frere [Philips van Dorp is in 1627 Willem Haultain opgevolgd als luitenant-admiraal van Zeeland]. N'apprehende rien quoyqu'ilz tardent; son merite luy en a desjà despesché la commission au coeur des gens de bien, et les meschans ne seront jamais capables de l'en effacer. Ce frere vault largement les autres, quelque impression que vous ayez du cadet [Arend van Dorp]. Cettuyci s'est insinué trop avant en ma cognoissance, desjà devant que ses comportements me fussent autres qu'indifferens, pour me faire soubscrire au jugement que vous en faictes par amour ou par charité. S'il a les bonnes parties que vous en imaginez, je veux bion m'en resjouïr aveq vous, mais si aussi je tesmoigne n'ignorer point le surprix de ses imperfections, je demande que vous n'en attribuyiez rien à la passion ou à un fol ressentiment de la folie qu'il a voulu employer contre moy. Car de faict, je tascheray tousjours à me tenir aussi lin de reven[che] qu'il a tesmoingné l'estre de la discretion. Outre que mon inclination naturelle me porte à cette resolution, pouvant bien me vanter de par la grace de Dieu, comme il y a en Sa parole, *qu'il m'est éscheu une bonne ame*, la consideration de cette alliance est assez capable de me persuader à la paix et à cette concorde où il faict si beau veoir freres uniz s'entretenir. Mais depuis que dernierement je vous en enseignay la voye aisée et ouverte, j'ay souvent pl[aint] à par moy d'avoir veu comme vous eustes peu agreable d'apprehender mes raisons. Je prie Dieu qu'il ne cesse de vous illuminer de son saint esprit, comme estant à tousjours de bon coeur

den Song.
Amsterdam, 2 Mars 1627.

Index

negotiations (of Constantijn Huygens
   to buy items) 47, 52–3
neo-classical, *see* architecture
Netherlands 2, 3, 7, 9, 11, 21, 22, 45,
   46, 48, 85, 86, 87
networks
   of Constantijn Huygens 45–64, 65
New Historicism 94
Newton, Sir Isaac 20, 24–5, 28–32
nine-ribbed lute 61–2
North Holland 2–3, 6–7, 11–13
North Sea 48

Oldenburg, Henry 41–3
Ottenheym, Koen 54

painters 12, 53, 69
Paludanus, Doctor 12
Paradoxia Epidemica 88, 90
Paris 23, 41, 63
Pembroke, Earl of 25–6
pendulum 36, 40, 42
   circular 41–3
   clocks 33–5, 39, 41–4
Pepys, Samuel 36–40
Philosophical Transactions 34
pirates 33–44
play, the play-element (in cultures) 85,
   90–92, 93, 94, 95, 99–100, 101
poets 1, 46, 49, 68, 69, 75
Principia 24–5
Protestants 7, 31–2
Public Record Office 6, 10, 15

'Reasons of misrule' 84, 87–8, 90–2, 94
relationships
   of Constantijn Huygens and
      Dorothea van Dorp 65–83
   of Constantijn Huygens and
      Margaret Croft 6
   of Constantijn Huygens and Mary
      Killigrew 76
   of Christiaan Huygens and Isaac
      Newton 30
   epistolary 74
   of Jane Carlyle and Geraldine
      Jewsbury 16

literary 66–9
   of Margaret Croft and Henry Erskine
      5–6
   web of 64
remarriage
   of Mary Killigrew to Sir Thomas
      Stafford 75
   in *Hamlet* 94
Rembrandt 64
Renaissance 86, 90, 93, 95
Renaissance Self-Fashioning 94
Restoration 15
Return of Martin Guerre, The 86, 92–3
Roemers, Anna, *see* Visscher, Anna
      Roemers
de Rols, Bertrande 92
Romein, Jan 88
Royal African Company 34
Royal Library, The Hague 1
Royal Society 20, 25, 28, 31, 33–4,
   36–9, 41–3
Royalton-Kisch, Martin 8
Rubens 52–4, 56

Saint Thomas (island) 33, 38
Salisbury 25–6
salons 68–9
science
   Anglo-Dutch collaboration and
      competition in 42–4
   the new science 32
   William III's lack of interest in 22,
      31–2
scientific virtuosi 30
scientists 18, 20, 49, 75, *see also* Sir
      Isaac Newton
sea-trials (of longitude/pendulum
      clocks) 34–5, 39, 43–4
Second World War 88
self-fashioning 65, 68, 88, 93–4, 100
separation (of Constantijn Huygens
      and Dorothea van Dorp) 71–2
serio ludere 91, 95
ships 18, 33, 37–9
Snouckaert, Maarten 46–8
social anthropology 86, 92
social history 91–2, 94